I0831497

# E-learning in English Medium Instruction (EMI): Academic language for university students

# Linguistic Insights

Studies in Language and Communication

Edited by Maurizio Gotti,
Emeritus Professor,
University of Bergamo, (Italy)

Volume 294

PETER LANG
Bern · Berlin · Bruxelles · New York · Oxford

Ana María Piquer-Píriz

# E-learning in English Medium Instruction (EMI): Academic language for university students

PETER LANG
Bern · Berlin · Bruxelles · New York · Oxford

**Bibliographic information published by die Deutsche Nationalbibliothek**
Die Deutsche Nationalbibliothek lists this publication in the Deutsche Nationalbibliografie; detailed bibliographic data is available on the Internet at ‹http://dnb.d-nb.de›.

Library of Congress Cataloging-in-Publication Data
A CIP catalog record for this book has been applied for at the Library of Congress.

The materials and the rest of the contents described in this book have been developed under the research project 'Diseño de entornos virtuales de aprendizaje colaborativo para la enseñanza integrada de contenidos y lenguas extranjeras (AICLE) en la Educación Superior adaptados a la Universidad de Extremadura (ICLUEx)' – 'Developing virtual collaborative learning environments for content and language integrated learning (CLIL) in Higher Education adapted to the University of Extremadura' (project number: IB18055), Junta de Extremadura European Regional Development Fund – ERDF.

Consejería de Economía, Ciencia y Agenda Digital

Fondo Europeo de Desarrollo Regional
Una manera de hacer Europa

ISSN 1424-8689
E-ISBN 978-3-0343-4628-3 (E-PDF)
DOI 10.3726/b20195
ISBN 978-3-0343-4589-7 (Print)
E-ISBN 978-3-0343-4629-0 (EPUB)

# Table of contents

# List of tables

# Acknowledgements

The materials and the rest of the contents described in this book have been developed under the research project '*Diseño de entornos virtuales de aprendizaje colaborativo para la enseñanza integrada de contenidos y lenguas extranjeras (AICLE) en la Educación Superior adaptados a la Universidad de Extremadura (ICLUEx)*' – 'Developing virtual collaborative learning environments for content and language integrated learning (CLIL) in Higher Education adapted to the University of Extremadura' (project number: IB18055), Junta de Extremadura European Regional Development Fund – ERDF.

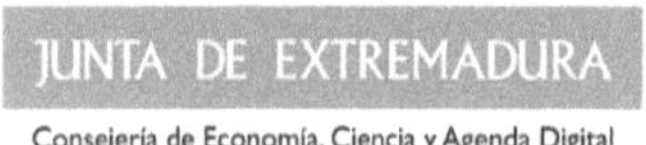


Fondo Europeo de Desarrollo Regional
Una manera de hacer Europa

I would like to express my gratitude to the entire ICLUEx project team[1] including Rafael Alejo, Irene Castellano, Marta Martín, Laura Fielden, Juan de Dios Martínez, Lucía Blázquez, Cecilia Calderón and Ana Pérez) for their invaluable contribution to the successful development of the project and its outcomes. I would also like to extend my thanks to the lecturers and students from the university of Extremadura who have inspired the design and participated in the piloting of the seven learning modules that make up this book, which I hope will be useful to other lecturers and students involved in the process of teaching and learning disciplinary content through English at university settings.

Lastly, I am also very grateful to James McCue for assistance in language editing.

Responsibility for the information and views expressed in the publication lies entirely with the author.

1 https://l2earnuex.wixsite.com/icluex/research-team

# Introduction

This book focuses on helping university students with some of the linguistic issues that they face when confronted with learning in English in their graduate or post-graduate degree programmes.

The use of English to teach content subjects in Higher Education has risen significantly over the last 20 years (Wächter & Maiworm 2014) and has been accompanied by a steadily growing research production (see Macaro 2018, 2022, for a review). Both strong points and difficulties in this practice have been identified. In relation to the latter, the shortage of adequate materials for teaching through a second language has been a recurrent issue in the research literature, in general, (Mehisto et al. 2008) and has been specifically emphasized by Higher Education lecturers (Aguilar & Rodríguez 2012; Pérez-Cañado 2020, 2021; Piquer-Píriz & Castellano-Risco 2021). At the same time, Information and Communication Technology (ICT) has been depicted as a powerful ally when teaching contents through a second language (see Fernández-Fontecha 2008; Pérez Torres 2015; Piquer-Píriz et al. 2021 or Montaner-Villalba & Gimeno-Sanz 2021, for some examples). Nowadays, learning, particularly in university contexts, takes place in multiple environments: face-to-face in lecture halls, more reduced seminars or in more practical environments such as labs and also through learner mobility and immersion in work situations. But, apart from all these on-site contexts, learning can also take place online. Thus, learners receive different kinds of input, not only from their lecturers but also from their peers, and there is also a constant flow of information on the internet through social media and multiple technologies that can be put at the service of effective methodologies.

Furthermore, in contexts in which English is used as Medium of Instruction (EMI), students would particularly need to develop their academic English in order to cope efficiently with the disciplinary contents that are presented to them in a language that is not their mother tongue.

This book intends to assist EMI students with their linguistic needs by offering online, self-study resources for university students enrolled in English-Taught Programmes (ETP) in which disciplinary subjects are taught through the medium of English. It offers a package of self-study resources consisting of seven modules for university students that were designed after conducting specific research into EMI students' linguistic needs in terms of academic genres, and discursive functions. These outputs derived from a funded research project, '*Developing virtual collaborative learning environments for content and language integrated learning (CLIL) in Higher Education adapted to the University of Extremadura*'[2]. The needs analysis served as the basis for the design and development of the materials included in the book. Seven modules were designed on the following topics: Creating outlines, concept maps, writing definitions, writing summaries, reporting data, the language of presentations and writing abstracts. All these modules were piloted with students in different degree programmes at the University of Extremadura (see Table 3, on page 31). The piloting confirmed the suitability of the materials for EMI undergraduate as well as postgraduate learners and the benefits of following a genre-based approach in this specific context.

The book starts with a brief theoretical introduction to two relevant, interrelated notions regarding learning through English at university: the process of internationalization of Higher Education Institutions (HEIs) and the role of academic language in university contexts. The second part of the book is devoted to seven modules designed to help university students involved in EMI programmes to improve their academic skills in English: Creating outlines, concept maps, writing definitions, writing summaries, reporting data, the language of presentations and writing abstracts. The modules have been sequenced according to their level of difficulty (from the easiest to the most complex), so for novice learners it is recommended to follow the established order.

2 *Diseño de entornos virtuales de aprendizaje colaborativo para la enseñanza integrada de contenidos y lenguas extranjeras (AICLE) en la Educación Superior adaptados a la Universidad de Extremadura (ICLUEx)*, project number IB18055, Junta de Extremadura and European Regional Development Fund – ERDF (project website: https://l2earnuex.wixsite.com/icluex)

However, each module is independent of the others (although there are some relationships between some of them that are highlighted) and has its own entity and can, therefore, be used in isolation according to the interests and needs of each learner. For each module, there is an introductory section that includes an overview and its main aims, followed by the expected learning outcomes. The contents of each module are presented, divided into phases and tasks, and a rubric for assessment is also included. At the end of the book, an answer key for all the proposed tasks is provided.

# 1. Some relevant theoretical notions

## 1.1. The process of internationalization of Higher Education Institutions

### *1.1.1 The European Higher Education Area (EHEA)*

Concern for internationalization among European universities is widely spread, with varying degrees of development, throughout the continent. Among the main objectives set by the European Union (EU) are respect for linguistic diversity, promotion of scientific and technological processes, promotion of economic and social cohesion, and free movement of citizens. In achieving these goals, which have a direct impact on increasing the employability of university graduates in the common space that makes up the EU, universities have an important mission.

The current structure of university studies in Europe, as is well known, is the result of the European Higher Education Area (EHEA)[3] initiative, which currently comprises 49 member countries[4].

The foundations of this new educational area were laid down in the Bologna Declaration (1999), which was an agreement signed by the Ministers of Education of 29 European countries (members of the European Union or in the process of accession), and based on convergence and cooperation in the field of higher education, in which the following main objectives were established:

3 For further information, please visit http://www.ehea.info/

4 See http://ehea.info/page-members, for specific information.

1. The adoption of a clear and easily comparable degree system with the aim of promoting the employability of students and the competitiveness of the European higher education system on an international level.
2. The implementation of a degree system based on two fundamental stages: a Bachelor's degree (degrees of a minimum duration of three years offering a level of qualification adequate for the European labour market) and a postgraduate degree (including Master's and Doctoral studies).
3. The establishment of the ECTS credit system, which stands for European Credit Transfer System. The main purpose of this new credit system is to promote student mobility. These credits are based on the learning outcomes and workload of a course and therefore students can transfer their ECTS credits, which would be added to the specific training programme of their choice, from one university to another.
4. The promotion of mobility of students, by facilitating their access to studies and other training opportunities and related services; and of teaching, research and administrative staff, through the recognition of research, teaching and training stays in European contexts.
5. The promotion of European cooperation in quality assurance, with particular emphasis on the development of comparable criteria and methodologies.
6. The promotion of a European dimension in higher education, in particular with regard to curriculum development, cooperation between institutions, mobility programmes and integrated training and research programmes.

Since the Bologna declaration, a series of meetings were established to follow up the process. These meetings have so far taken place in Prague (2001), Berlin (2003), Bergen (2005), London (2007), Leuven (2009), Budapest and Vienna (2010), Bucharest (2012), Yerevan (2015), Paris (2018) and Rome – virtual (2020). The EHEA ministerial conference held online in 2020 during the Coronavirus pandemic acknowledged how universities organized 'online emergency pedagogies', at the time, switching to digital education and reorganizing their teaching-learning and assessment policies. Digital education proved its ability to offer quality and accessible provision for use in emergency situations, and that it should be further explored in relation to possibilities for international learning experiences that could be physical, blended or online, ensuring a wider, more accessible, and sustainable sharing of knowledge.

### *1.1.2 'Internationalization abroad' vs. 'internationalization at home'*

Thus, for more than two decades, European policies have been promoting the internationalization of their Higher Education Institutions. Knight (1993, p. 21) provided a general definition of the concept of internationalization as *"the process of integrating an international/intercultural dimension into the teaching, research and service functions of the institution"* that she later updated to explicitly include the context in which it was set, i.e., tertiary education: *"the process of integrating an international, intercultural, or global dimension into the purpose, functions or delivery of postsecondary education"* (2004, p. 11).

In 2015, de Wit et al. revisited Knight's definition by adding a final consideration about its important function: "*the intentional process of integrating an international, intercultural or global dimension into the purpose, functions and delivery of post-secondary education, in order to enhance the quality of education and research for all students and staff, and to make a meaningful contribution to society*" (p. 29). More recently, two key aspects that should lead the development of the process of internationalization currently and in the future have been also emphasized: first, the importance of adopting a student-centred perspective, one of its main outcomes being that learners should attain international awareness and intercultural competence (Coelen 2016); and, secondly, the fact that it is essential to expand the scope of internationalization to encompass all stakeholders involved in the process. As de Wit and Deca (2020, p. 7) put it "*the shift from internationalization abroad with a strong focus on a small elite of mobile students, faculty, administrators and programs towards internationalization at home for all students, faculty and administrators is even more urgent than ever.*" In this sense, Beelen & Jones's (2015) distinction between what has been called 'internationalization abroad' -where Erasmus programmes are primarily targeted- and 'internationalization at home' -where programmes using English as Medium of Instruction ('EMI programmes') play an important role- proves useful. Both programmes are key to the internationalization processes of most European universities (Sursock 2015) and aim to respond to the challenges of a new, highly competitive, knowledge-based economic landscape in which students are required to develop competences and skills that enable them to actively participate in the development of this new society.

Beelen and Jones (2015, p. 61) defined 'internationalization abroad' as "*all forms of education across borders*". In contrast, 'internationalization at home' consists of a series of practices devoted to carrying out activities that help students develop international understanding and intercultural skills while at universities in their home country (Beelen & Jones 2015; Knight 2005). In Beelen & Jones's words (2015, p. 69), 'internationalization at home' is "*the purposeful integration of international and intercultural dimensions into the formal and informal curriculum for all students within domestic learning environments*". Thus, within this new approach to internationalization, HEIs commit themselves to promoting an international and cross-cultural academic environment for all the members of the community, including students, lecturers, and other staff members. This commitment extends to both mobility programmes abroad and internal, on-campus policies with the aim of integrating international perspectives into teaching-learning curricular activities, research and service activities. To achieve these challenging aims within the domestic environment, the development of language skills in an academic context and aided by technology-enabled methodologies can be of great significance. This book aims to make a contribution in the same vein as some previous publications such as the book by Pérez-Cañado and Ojeda-Pinar (2018) on communicative classroom language in Content and Language Integrated Learning (CLIL) contexts or Lasagabaster, Doiz, Gómez-Lacabex and Kopinska (2021) that offers EMI students of History rich materials that will help them to adapt their discourse to the language of their disciplinary area.

### *1.1.3 English as the language of communication in the academic world*

Concerning the development of language skills, the role of English as a 'lingua franca' for communication in the academic world (Mauranen 2012) has led to its increasing integration as a key element in the different internationalization initiatives in HEIs (Doiz et al. 2013). This is reflected in different measures taken to encourage its use, ranging from the promotion of specific 'English language' or 'English for specific purposes' subjects to the so-called 'Bilingual Degrees' or 'European Degrees', in which specific subjects (e.g. Biology, Chemistry, Economics or Psychology) are taught in English by lecturers specialising in these fields of knowledge. The significant rise in both the number of such programmes -increased by 239% within a period of 7 years (2007–2014)- and the number of students enrolling in them in Europe confirms this trend (Wächter & Maiworm 2014). As Macaro et al. (2019) put it, resorting to English as the language of communication in the classroom, i.e., using EMI, is one of the main ways for European HEIs to enhance their international profile and to attract students and staff from other countries. Some of the main characteristics of EMI programmes (cf. Pecorari and Malmström 2018) are the following: first, English is the second language (L2) for most participants (both students and lecturers) in this type of programmes ('internationalization at home'). Secondly, English itself is not usually a subject taught in the programme (it is not EFL) but rather it is the language used for instruction purposes (it is EMI). And thirdly, unlike in Content and Language Integrated (CLIL) programmes which are more common in earlier educational stages (primary and secondary education) and advocate an explicit language focus, in EMI programmes, the teaching of content and not language maintains the predominant role, and the L2 is perceived by lecturers - who are not language specialists but experts on disciplinary contents- as a communication tool that is commonly used in their field of expertise and will be beneficial for their students in their future careers. They expect some incidental L2 learning as a result of the use of English in their classes but, in most cases, they neither plan nor assess linguistic outcomes. A broader perspective to this phenomenon has been recently advocated by Dafouz & Smit (2016, 2020) who have coined the term EME (English Medium Education) and EMEMUS (English-Medium

Education in Multilingual University Settings) which they define as conceptually wider and more inclusive than previous accounts since a broader sociolinguistic multilingual context including languages other than English is set up and various research and pedagogical approaches are included.

Finally, another trend argues for a more balanced content-language learning approach in university settings. The acronym 'Integrating Content and Language in Higher Education' (ICLHE) has been specifically coined to refer to CLIL in tertiary education (Wilkinson 2018) and the 'clil-ization' of EMI programmes at universities both from a theoretical perspective (Alejo-González 2018; Pérez-Cañado 2020) and in more practical ways (Morgado et al. 2015; Morgado et al. 2020) has been proposed.

From any of these perspectives, although to different extents, it seems clear that being able to communicate in English in an academic context is one of those key skills for internationalization (both at home and abroad) that HEIs are aiming to offer their students to ensure their development, autonomy, and employability. The next section is specifically devoted to the role of academic language in university settings.

## 1.2. Academic language in university contexts

### *1.2.1 From academic language to academic literacies*

University students are expected to use language appropriate for study, both in their L1 and, as has been discussed in the previous section, often, also in English, especially, if they decide to enroll in EMI programmes. Cummins's (1979, 2017) well-known distinction between BICS (Basic Interpersonal Communicative Skills) and CALP (Cognitive Academic Language Proficiency) illustrates the different kinds of language people use every day in social interactions (BICS) as opposed to the specialized language they need to develop to function in academic contexts (CALP). When children begin their education at school, they become exposed to a type of language which is quite distanced from what they are used to in their family environment. As Schleppegrell (2006, p. 49) points out: "*In understanding academic language, the focus is on the fact that students are expected to read, write and speak at school using language that presents knowledge that is formal, technical, and distanced from everyday life [. . .] different from the informal language that is so familiar to children [when] they interact in their homes and communities.*" Furthermore, academic language is challenging and an adequate development of it may be crucial for learners' successful educational progress. Teachers, especially at the initial and intermediate stages, can play a key role in this process: "*If teachers are aware of the challenges in the language itself, children from backgrounds where they experience little language use that is "academic" outside of school can be empowered through an appropriate pedagogy to learn subject matter that is presented in challenging language*" (Schleppegrell 2006, p. 49). For her, this 'language of schooling' (Schleppegrell 2004) is expected to display knowledge, organize information and be authoritative, and it is dense, abstract and technical, it often includes multiple semiotic systems, and it is expected to follow certain conventional structures and to have an appropriate 'voice'.

Inculturation into correct use of academic language becomes more complex as students progress through their academic life, and it is even more challenging if they have to do it in English when English is not their native language. In fact, since the mid-1970s, there is an approach devoted to academic language, known as English for Academic Purposes (EAP) which some authors (e.g. Swales 1995) considered, in its beginnings, as a branch of the broader field of English for Specific Purposes (ESP) or, even more generally speaking, a part of English Language Teaching (ELT). EAP has grown enormously since then, partly due to the internationalization of higher education that, as mentioned above, has been accompanied by an increasing use of English as the language of academic knowledge exchange.

Chamot and O'Malley (1994) provided a definition of academic English that took into consideration both teachers and students, as well as its purpose in acquiring new skills and knowledge, and described some of its main features such as conveying new information, describing abstract ideas and developing students' conceptual understanding.

In a more recent account of EAP, Hyland (2006, p. 1) stated that: *"EAP has expanded with the growth of university places in many countries and increasing numbers of international students undertaking tertiary studies in English"*. As a result, *"EAP is now situated at the front line of both theory development and innovative practice in teaching English as a second/other language"*. Among other things, he emphasized two important issues that EAP should address nowadays: (1) the new roles students must take on and the new ways for them to engage with knowledge in higher education; and (2) the fact that not all academic disciplines share uniform communication practices but rather construct knowledge in different ways. This latter aspect relates to the combination of three main types of language in an EMI class: disciplinary language (the language that Hyland is referring to and which is the specific language of each field of expertise – e.g. the language of History, Physics, Education or Biology – and differs greatly between disciplines not only in the use of specific terminology but also in the genres employed), everyday language (which is usually employed to link new concepts with learners' previous knowledge, Cummins's BICS) and academic language (which is cross-curricular and, therefore, commonly shared in all disciplines, Cummins's CALP). This book focuses on the latter: the type of language that is useful for any university student regardless of their discipline of study. It is also concerned with the new roles that students must take on and the new ways for them to engage with knowledge. In this sense, there are two basic principles that underlie the design of the modules presented in the next section: online learning and self-directed learning. Online learning is understood here as learning in a remote, digital environment which, in the case of the proposed materials, includes digital learning content and interactive learning experiences for the students. Self-directed learning is advocated as a method of knowledge acquisition through which learners direct their own learning, usually outside the classroom and without direct guidance or supervision by the teacher. The modules are designed to encourage learner autonomy, with each assignment providing a key or model answer to test and evaluate their own productions. This also means that lecturers do not need to devote excessive class time to linguistic content and can focus on their own disciplinary content.

A final notion that has been recently developed and, in my view, is also very relevant to understand academic language at university contexts at present is that of 'academic literacies' which refer to the skills that students need to develop in order to function in their disciplinary communities. These skills not only include the reading and writing of academic texts but also the ability to interact with other members of the academic community by sharing ideas and following the expected conventions of the discipline (Lea 2004, 2017). Lea (2017, p. 148) highlights that *"literacy is not a unitary skill that can be transferred with ease from context to context. The research points to the requirement for students to switch between many different types of written text, as they encounter new modules or courses and the writing demands of different disciplinary genres, departments, and academic staff"*.

### *1.2.2 EMI students' perceived language needs*

In order to help EMI students develop their academic English, the first step would be to explore their needs. Unlike the case of EMI lecturers' where there is an incipient line of research devoted to analysing their needs (Coelho 2022; Gustafsson 2020; Morell & Volchenkova 2021, Pérez-Cañado 2016, 2020, 2021; Piquer-Píriz & Castellano-Risco 2021), the needs of students have been explored to a much lesser extent (Aguilar & Rodríguez 2012; Pérez-Cañado 2021). As a previous step to the design of the materials, the linguistic needs of EMI students from the University of Extremadura were analysed. A quantitative questionnaire (adapted from Pérez-Cañado 2020) and structured around three main areas, i.e., linguistic competence, methodology and materials, and continuous training, was administered to 155 learners from different disciplinary areas. It consisted of 45 items referring not only to students' linguistic competence but also to their perceptions about their lecturers' language skills, and it also included a section in which students were asked about their assessment practices in their EMI programmes.

The analysis of the results (presented in Table 1) showed that the area in which students perceived their language knowledge was lowest was that related to academic vocabulary, and their greatest perceived needs were related to more training in oral skills not only for communicating in class but also for public speaking when delivering oral presentations, together with the need to improve their knowledge of the specific vocabulary of their fields of expertise.

**Table 1.** EMI students' language knowledge perception vs. perceived needs

| **Lowest knowledge perception** | **vs.** | **Greatest perceived needs** | | |
|---|---|---|---|---|
| My knowledge of academic vocabulary in English is adequate | | I need more training in oral skills to communicate with my classmates and lecturers in the EMI classes. | I need more training in the specific vocabulary of my area of expertise | I need more training in preparing oral presentations and public speaking |
| Min.: 1.000<br>**Mean: 2.897**<br>Max.: 4.000 | | Min.: 1.000<br>**Mean: 2.716**<br>Max.: 4.000 | Min.: 1.000<br>**Mean: 2.858**<br>Max.: 4.000 | Min.: 1.000<br>**Mean: 2.794**<br>Max.: 4.000 |

Chapter 2 presents the seven modules that I hope will help university students from any discipline to improve their academic English. They range from some basic functions (such as creating outlines and concept maps or writing definitions and summaries), which university students are expected to do as part of the work required in their study programmes, to more advanced notions such as being able to report data, deliver an oral presentation or write scientific abstracts.

# 2. Helping EMI students with academic language: Seven modules to develop academic literacies

This section presents a package of self-study resources which includes seven modules that can also be completed online, and which have been designed to aid university students enrolled in EMI programmes with their linguistic needs in order to fulfil the requirements of the subjects they study in English.

Table 2 shows the basic information related to each of the modules including their title, the linguistics skills that are worked on in each of them, the number of phases they comprise, the estimated time needed to complete them, and the links to an introductory video for each of them in the 'YouTube' channel 'Language Education and Research Work (L2EARN)'[5]. There is also an interactive version of each module in the web-based tool 'Genially'[6] where students will find all the information needed to complete each module online: phases, tasks, model answers and the self-assessment questionnaires.

5 To visit the YouTube channel 'Language Education and Research Work (L2EARN)', please use the following link: https://www.youtube.com/@languageeducationandresear6733

6 *Genially* is a web-based tool for creating interactive content. It is available in a free version and used worldwide with great acceptance in the educational community. For further information, visit https://genial.ly/we-are/

**Table 2.** A summary of the modules and their main features

| Module | Linguistic skills | Phases | Estimated time | Links |
|---|---|---|---|---|
| **0. Introductory module: Creating outlines** | Oral and written comprehension Written production | 4 | 4-5 hours | **YouTube video** https://youtu.be/C5Kw rK0nOWA **Genially** https://view.genial.ly/ 60363e6de9246f0d 8408d047/learning-experience-didactic-unit-creating-outlinesmodule |
| **Concept maps** | Oral and written comprehension | 4 | 3 hours | **YouTube video** https://youtu.be/HExi 8WXtQd8 **Genially** https://view.genial.ly/ 6040aa0545e4040d2 f09f9c9/learning-experience-didactic-unit-concept-maps-moduleicluex |
| **2. Writing definitions** | Oral and written comprehension Written production | 5 | 6 hours | **YouTube video** https://youtu.be/I2S1 spAdMk4 **Genially** https://view.genial.ly/ 60467d4030d8a70d 14c69f87/learning-experience-didactic-unit-writing-definitionsmodule |
| **3. Writing summaries** | Oral and written comprehension Written production | 4 | 3 ½ hours | **YouTube video** https://youtu.be/UXje hxyA4CU **Genially** https://view.genial.ly/ 5fd9d1a43c971e0d 6598c81b/learning-experience-didactic-unit-writing-summariesmodule |

**Table 2.** Continued

| Module | Linguistic skills | Phases | Estimated time | Links |
|---|---|---|---|---|
| **4. Reporting data** | Oral and written comprehension Written production | 4 | 4-5 hours | **YouTube video** I https://youtu.be/iUKl44062OA YouTube video II https://youtu.be/9CslIdoicYI **Genially** https://view.genial.ly/605867e01e77ea0d0e1d3e92/learning-experience-didactic-unit-reporting-datamodule |
| **5. The language of presentations** | Oral and written comprehension Written production | 5 | 5-6 hours | **YouTube video** https://youtu.be/g7i3I6wyhIU **Genially** https://view.genial.ly/5ffd6ec236185d5bd50d1eec/learning-experience-didactic-unit-the-language-of-presentationsmodule |
| **6. Writing abstracts** | Oral and written comprehension Written production | 4 | 3-4 hours | **YouTube video** https://youtu.be/h0pVQGWcm1M **Genially** https://view.genial.ly/606ac8630a2eda0ce859918c/learning-experience-didactic-unit-writing-abstractsmodule |

Before looking at the modules themselves, Section 2.1 briefly discusses the main methodological principles used in their design.

## 2.1. Methodology

The methodology employed in the design of the modules followed the usual methodological steps required for the development of e-learning educational materials, which are as follows:

### *2.1.1. Needs Analysis (NA)*

As mentioned above, the first step was an analysis of the students' needs that comprised three stages:

**1. Target situation analysis**

Starting from the Target Situation Analysis and following the idea of the Communication Needs Processor (CNP) advocated by Munby (1978), the following aspects were analysed and taken into consideration in the data collection process:

1. participants on whom the NA is performed (our EMI students)
2. purposive domain, which is equivalent to the field of specialisation (academic English used by non-native speakers)
3. setting or characteristics of the physical and psychosocial environment in which the L2 is going to be used (L2 classes where English is used as Medium of Instruction)
4. interaction, which identifies those with whom the participant is going to communicate as well as the roles that each one will play in the interaction (T-S but also S-S interaction)
5. instrumentality, which in turn is determined by three concepts: (a) medium (spoken/written/productive/receptive) through which communication takes place (the ones established by the CEFR); (b) mode (e.g. written and spoken), and (c) channel, which indicates the material medium through which communication takes place (face-to-face and online)
6. dialect, which specifies what kind of dialect form is required (English as a Lingua Franca)

7. target level, which specifies the level of L2 proficiency (B2 level in English as described in the CEFR)
8. communicative event or concrete act in which communication takes place (academic context).

## 2. Present situation analysis

In this step, the information is provided by the target students themselves, by the institution where the course will take place or even by the teachers.

The information required from the learners for this type of analysis is mainly related to their level of mastery of the different skills, their strengths and weaknesses in the structures, and also their learning experiences. The profile obtained from this analysis gives us the guidelines for adequate programming in which the needs of the learner, understood in this way, are covered. From this, we established a questionnaire (adapted from the validated questionnaire used by Pérez-Cañado 2020) in which the linguistic activities (target events) that could be carried out in the target situation are listed. This initial list allowed learners to express their opinion on the real need for these activities in the future, as well as their current level of knowledge. See Section 1.2.2 (pp.23–24) for further details on this.

## 3. Strategic analysis

Hutchinson and Waters (1987) postulate the need to identify not only the behaviours or activities that learners must carry out in the target situation, but fundamentally the strategies that will enable them to learn to function in the target situation. The emphasis is therefore on how to acquire this final repertoire, and the path to be taken in order to achieve it (learning needs). For this, it was necessary to carry out a means analysis, i.e., what materials and resources are available and accessible so that learners can meet their needs. It is important to point out that Holliday and Cooke (1982) and Holliday (1994, 1995) emphasize that it is not desirable to import teaching models that are alien to the local culture, which means that many academic English materials, whose target students are students who are going to enrol in British or American universities, may not be strictly useful for EMI students. We opted for open, free platforms (YouTube) and web-based tools (Genially) that are accessible for any student and can be used not only on their computers but also on mobile devices. The introductory videos were voiced by a non-native speaker of English who uses a variety of the language that would correspond to international English as the context is that of English as a Lingua Franca (ELF).

### *2.1.2. Design of materials*

Once the Needs Analysis was carried out in depth, as established in the previous stage, the steps for the design of materials were set up, from the general to the specific:

1. The linguistic objectives to be covered by the design of materials and which are connected to the linguistic needs noted in the previous section were established.
2. The tasks and exercises that respond to the attainment of the linguistic objectives set were designed.
3. Appropriate IT tools for each set of objectives identified were selected.
4. The structure of the digital materials and the design of a coherent overall outline for their production were developed.
5. Multimedia scripts to make up the content of the digital resource for each of the modules were prepared. The scripts were adaptations of the material we had identified in the Needs Analysis, so learners could check the immediate usefulness in their learning context of using the digital material we developed.
6. The multimedia product was elaborated, tested, and revised.
7. A pilot experiment was carried out and, from its findings, some modifications were made to the final version.
8. The modules were implemented with students enrolled in undergraduate and postgraduate degree courses at the university of Extremadura (Spain).

9. A didactic manual (Piquer-Píriz et al. 2022) was produced which included guidelines for the educational use of the multimedia material.

The modules were implemented at different undergraduate programmes and a postgraduate programme at the university of Extremadura in the academic years 2020–21, 2021–22, as shown in Table 3.

**Table 3.** Implementation of the modules at the University of Extremadura (academic years 2020–21, 2021–22)

| Module | Degree programme/s |
|---|---|
| 0. Introductory module: Creating outlines | • Degree in English Studies<br>• Master in Bilingual Education through English for Primary and Secondary School Teachers |
| 1. Concept maps | • Degree in Primary Education |
| 2. Writing definitions | • Degree in Primary Education (bilingual)<br>• Degree in English Studies |
| 3. Writing summaries | • Master in Bilingual Education through English for Primary and Secondary School Teachers |
| 4. Reporting data | • Degree in Economy<br>• Degree in Business Administration and Management<br>• Degree in Chemistry<br>• Degree in Oenology |
| 5. The language of presentations | • Degree in Economy<br>• Degree in Business Administration and Management |

Some of the groups were administered a pre-test and a post-test in which they had to complete the final task of each module that was assessed with the rubric designed for each of them. As shown in Table 4, the results were positive in all cases (marked with * for a significant improvement at the rate 0.05 and ** for a significant improvement at the 0.01 level).

**Table 4.** Results from the piloting of the modules

| Module | Piloted in | N | Pre-test (out of 10) | Post-test (out of 10) | Result |
|---|---|---|---|---|---|
| Introductory module: creating outlines | Degree in English Studies | 76 | 6.96 | 7.94 | 0.98** |
| Writing definitions | Degree in Primary Education (bilingual) | 77 | 3.55 | 4.19 | 0.64** |
| Writing summaries | Master in Bilingual Education through English for Primary and Secondary School Teachers | 12 | 5.62 | 6.52 | 0.90** |
| Reporting data | Degree in Economy | 47 | 4.06 | 7.26 | 3.20** |
| The language of presentations | Degree in Economy | 41 | 5.55 | 7.25 | 1.7** |

## 2.2. Modules

### *2.2.1. Introductory module: Creating outlines*

#### **2.2.1.1. Overview and aims**

This module aims to provide students with the fundamental knowledge and tools to create outlines. An outline is usually described as a general plan of the material that is going to be used for a written piece of work or an oral presentation. In this sense, it is a very important first step for productive tasks. However, outlines can also be understood, from a receptive perspective, as a way of efficiently sketching the most relevant information of a text. These types of outlines are often called 'summary outlines' as they may be the first step to write a summary which is a longer, more complex piece of work. In EMI university contexts, students are very often asked to read papers or chapters written in English and being able to visually organise the key information they contain in a logical order to have it ready to see at a glance is a very useful technique. In this module, students will be given help to create this type of outlines first, in order to progressively move to the more creative outlines to plan their own productions.

This topic will be introduced over four different self-study phases, implementing both theoretical aspects and practical exercises under the principles of self-study and self-assessment. In short, the goal of this module is to provide the necessary knowledge about understanding and writing outlines.

The interactive version of the module developed in *Genial.ly* can be accessed here: https://view.genial.ly/60363e6de9246f0d8408d047/learning-experience-didactic-unit-creating-outlinesmodule

And the introductory video hosted in the *L2EARN* channel in YouTube is also freely available: https://youtu.be/C5KwrK0nOWA

At the end of this module, students will be able to:

- Create their own outline from any type of source
- Learn how to identify the main ideas, the supporting ideas, and the details of a text.
- Use the correct language structures to write an adequate outline.
- Self-assess their own performance at the end of each phase.

Additionally, students will be able to understand written input as well as produce written output related to the content objectives.

This module serves as an introduction, since outlines are the starting point for creating concept maps (module 1), for writing summaries (module 3) and for creating presentations (module 5). You can check the modules on these topics for further information.

Finally, the module is designed to be completed in 4 or 5 hours, so the student workload should not be longer than this. According to the Common European Framework of Reference (CEFR), it is adapted to B2 level (English), and will contribute to the development of the following skills: spoken comprehension, written comprehension, and written production.

### 2.2.1.2. Learning outcomes

The *language skills (CEFR)*[7] that are going to be deal with in this module are the following:

1. Comprehension:
   (a) Written:
      - Can scan quickly through long and complex texts, locating relevant details.
      - Can recognise different structures in discursive text: contrasting arguments, problem-solution presentation, and cause-effect relationships.

   (b) Spoken:
      - Can understand recordings in the standard form of the language likely to be encountered in social, professional, or academic life and identify speaker viewpoints and attitudes as well as the information content.
2. Production:
   (a) Written:
      - Can synthesise information and arguments from a number of sources.
      - Can write a detailed description of a complex process.

Apart from these linguistic competencies, there are other skills, related to the contents of the module, that are also developed:

- Identifying key ideas.
- Organising information.
- Outlining.

### 2.2.1.3. Contents: Phases and tasks

Table 5 shows the activities that are developed in the module.

7 In all the modules, the language skills were selected from those described in the CEFR original document (2001) as they are broader and clearer to a non-specialist audience and, therefore, more suitable for our audience: EMI students.

**Table 5.** List of activities for introductory module 'Creating outlines'

| Phase | Aim | Tasks | Description | Time | Typology |
|---|---|---|---|---|---|
| Phase 1 | To introduce what an outline is and its main characteristics and elements. | Task 1: video and questionnaire | *Presentation task*: first contact with outlines. | 30' | Listening |
| | | Task 2: checklist | *Assessment task*: perception checklist. | 5' | Reading |
| Phase 2 | To present the steps that should be carried out before creating an outline. Students will be asked to work with texts, identifying their main and supporting ideas, and details. | Task 3: classifying ideas | *Practice task*: differentiating between main ideas, supporting ideas and details of a text. | 45' | Reading |
| | | Task 4: checklist | *Assessment task*: perception checklist. | 5' | Reading |
| Phase 3 | To work with different types of outlines so that students discover their preferred way of displaying information. | Task 5: choosing your outline | *Practice task*: choosing their preferred type of outline (topic, sentence-verbal or sentence-visual outline) | 30'-40' | Reading |
| | | Task 6: checklist | *Assessment task*: perception checklist | 5' | Reading |
| Phase 4 | To assess students' ability to build their own outline, using apps to do so. | Task 7: creating your own outline | *Production task*: creating an outline from a text previously worked in class by using one of the proposed apps. | 1 ½ hour | Writing |
| | | Task 8: creative outline | *Production task:* creating an outline from a topic they decide. | 1 hour | Writing |
| | | Task 9: checklist | *Assessment*: perception checklist | 5' | Reading |

### *Phase 1: Warm-up*

The main learning goal of this phase is for students to become familiar with the basic aspects needed before creating an outline. This first step consists in learning what an outline is, what is needed to create an outline and the elements that should be included in it.

Phase 1 will be completed in 30 minutes through two different tasks:

- Task 1 is a presentation task to become familiar with outlines (listening activity).
- Task 2 is a checklist to assess understanding (reading activity).

In the presentation task (task 1), students will be asked to watch the introductory video about outlines (https://youtu.be/C5KwrK0nOWA) and answer a questionnaire comprising six multiple-choice questions. This will be the first time the concept of outlines is introduced.

In task 2, students can assess their own learning checking if they have properly understood the main ideas presented in the video.

**Task 1. Questionnaire on the theoretical video**

1. **What is an outline?**
   a. A skeleton that keeps ideas together in an organised way.
   b. A framework for presenting the ideas of a topic.
   c. Both of the above.
2. **Why should outlines be created?**
   a. To act as starting points for other productions.
   b. To summarise the information of a given text.
   c. After a summary or a presentation, as a recapping tool.
3. **An outline**…
   a. makes the learning process slower.
   b. contains an ordered overview of the information of a text.
   c. is not necessary to identify the main ideas of a text.
4. **Which one of these steps is NOT necessary for creating an outline?**
   a. Looking in the dictionary for words that you may not know.
   b. Beginning by writing what you think is the main idea of the reading selection.
   c. Distinguishing between supporting ideas and details.

5. **Which one of these is NOT a type of outline?**
   a. Sentence-verbal outline.
   b. Topic outline.
   c. Verbal-definition outline.
6. **Which of these factors is important to bear in mind when using online tools?**
   a. Automatic styling.
   b. Image fading.
   c. None of the above.

**Task 2. Checklist phase 1**

1. **I have learnt what an outline is**
   a. Yes
   b. No
2. **I have understood what should be included in an outline**
   a. Yes
   b. No
3. **I have learnt the steps to follow when creating an outline**
   a. Yes
   b. No
4. **I am familiar with online tools for creating outlines**
   a. Yes
   b. No

***Phase 2: Analysing texts***

The main aim of phase 2 is to provide some insights into the most common strategies for working with texts before creating outlines. Students will identify the main elements and characteristics of texts: main ideas, supporting points, details, and irrelevant information, as well as how to structure these before starting to write their outline.

Phase 2 will be developed in 1 hour through two different tasks:

- Task 3 is a practice task to identify the elements of an outline (reading activity).
- Task 4 is a checklist to assess understanding (reading activity).

In task 3, students will have to identify the information that should be included in an outline: the main and supporting ideas and the details of the text. After completing the task, they will be provided with a model answer (reading activity).

In task 4, students can assess their own learning checking if they have understood the contents of the phase.

**Task 3. Differentiating among the elements of a given text**

*Read the text "Developing CLIL students' writing: From oracy to literacy" (from Llinares et al., 2012, pp. 244–245) and identify the information that should be included in an outline (the main and supporting ideas and the details of the text). You can use the classification grid provided to complete this task.*

*When you finish, you can check your ideas with the model answer provided (different answers are possible).*

| Materials for Task 3. 'Differentiating among the elements of a given text' |
|---|

- **Text: Developing CLIL students' writing: From oracy to literacy**

"The role of writing as part of learning in CLIL contexts is, at present, largely unrecognised, with much more interest being shown in the development of oracy, being able to talk about subject content. Teaching and learning in the classroom are mainly carried out through talk, though support from other modes is brought in as the teacher turns to the use of board or screen, or students consult textbooks and other print materials. Support from the written mode is especially important, since it provides the students with both information and models of subject-specific language as they read. While the process of understanding text written in a foreign language demands considerable effort, that of writing a text in a foreign language requires much more. Writing involves decision making at different levels, from what is the purpose of writing – the genre – to what is the right word or structure for the meaning we want to make – that is, choices at the level of register. It also allows reflection, since it leaves a permanent trace for the writer to examine. The inclusion of writing tasks in CLIL classes can be seen as a way of enhancing the learning process.

This is because the activity of creating written text in the foreign language is an exercise which has value for a number of reasons.

Writing is not only useful to show what has been learned, but the process of writing leads to discovery and knowledge creation, as all writers know. Writing about content is, on the one hand, a way for students to find out what they know and don't know about what they have studied. It is also a way to develop and expand language resources in the foreign language. This has been shown in detailed studies of L2 writers during the actual process of writing a text. Researchers have analysed the points at which these students struggle with the foreign language, looking for lexical items, a grammatical structure or a reformulation which will really express the writer's ideas (e.g. Manchón et al. 2009; Roca et al. 2006). Their results have convinced them of the role of writing in learning a foreign language. Psychologists have found, too, that the effort involved in expressing meaning in a foreign language leads to deeper processing of content (Heine 2010). This means writing is also especially effective for the learning of content when this takes place in a foreign language.

Writing about subject content requires different choices from the linguistic system from those used for spoken classroom interaction. Even in L1, many students need help to learn the written registers of their subjects when they move into the disciplines at secondary school, and this is even more true for students studying in a foreign language. To support CLIL students in the transition from the spoken to the written mode in school subjects, there are different types of register scaffolding which can have beneficial effects on students' performance. On the one hand, there is planned register scaffolding at the macrolevel, or task scaffolding (Llinares and Whittaker 2009), in which the activities are sequenced, so that students first work in the spoken mode, building up knowledge of a topic area –that is, building a stable knowledge base from which to move into the more difficult written mode (Bereiter and Scardamalia, 1988) [. . .]. Besides this type of planned scaffolding, teachers can use spontaneous register scaffolding, at the microlevel [. . .] reformulating the students' spoken production to make it represent knowledge in more effective and academically acceptable ways."

**Source**: Llinares, A., T. Morton and R. Whittaker (2012). *The roles of language in CLIL*. Cambridge: Cambridge University Press. Chapter 8, pp. 244–245. Reproduced with permission of Cambridge University Press through PLSclear.

- Classification grid (template suitable for edition)

<table>
<tr><th>Main Idea</th><th>Supporting Ideas</th><th>Details</th></tr>
<tr><td rowspan="2"></td><td rowspan="2"></td><td></td></tr>
<tr><td></td></tr>
<tr><td></td><td rowspan="2"></td><td></td></tr>
<tr><td></td><td></td></tr>
<tr><td rowspan="2"></td><td rowspan="2"></td><td></td></tr>
<tr><td></td></tr>
<tr><td></td><td rowspan="2"></td><td></td></tr>
<tr><td></td><td></td></tr>
<tr><td></td><td rowspan="2"></td><td></td></tr>
<tr><td></td><td></td></tr>
<tr><td></td><td rowspan="3"></td><td></td></tr>
<tr><td></td><td></td></tr>
<tr><td></td><td></td></tr>
</table>

## Task 4. Checklist phase 2

1. **I have learnt how to identify the main elements of a text**
    a. Yes
    b. No
2. **I can distinguish between main and supporting ideas**
    a. Yes
    b. No
3. **I can identify the details of a supporting idea**
    a. Yes
    b. No

***Phase 3: Types of outlines***

The main learning objective of this phase is to become familiar with the different types of outlines and being able to use them according to the students' learning style.

Its duration will vary between 30 minutes and 1 hour, and will be developed through two different tasks:

- Task 5 is a practice task to present different types of outlines (reading activity).
- Task 6 is a checklist to assess understanding (reading activity).

In the practice task (task 5), the three types of outlines of the same text will be provided (topic, sentence-verbal and sentence-visual outlines). Students will be asked to choose their preferred one, justifying their choice (e.g., what is their preferred way of portraying information/ what is the most complete outline). For the development of this task, the following materials will be used: "Text 1: Developing CLIL students' writing" (presented above) and "Samples of different types of outlines" (see below).

In task 6, students can assess their own learning, checking if they have understood the contents of the phase.

**Task 5. Choosing your preferred type of outline**

*In this task, we are going to work with the same text as we did in task 3 (Text 1: "Developing CLIL students' writing: From oracy to literacy"). Below, there are three types of outlines of the text: a topic outline, a sentence-verbal outline and a sentence-visual outline.*

1. *Which one do you like the most?*
2. *Which one do you think portrays the information best?*
3. *Which one is most complete?*
4. *Would you add anything to them?*

## Materials for Task 5. 'Choosing your preferred type of outline'

- **Text 1: "Developing CLIL students' writing: From oracy to literacy" (see Task 3 above)**
- **Samples of different types of outlines (Figures 1, 2 and 3)**

### Outline 1. Topic outline

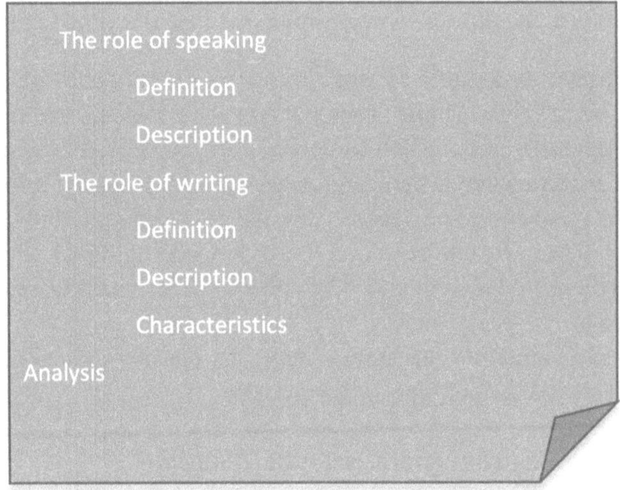


**Figure 1.** Topic outline. Source: Own elaboration

## Outline 2. Sentence-verbal outline

Outline: Developing CLIL students' writing: From oracy to literacy

THE ROLE OF SPEAKING

- ◊ Well-studied
- ◊ Teaching and learning through talk
- ◊ Ability to talk about subject content, supported by:
  - ✓ *screens*
  - ✓ *boards*
  - ✓ *textbooks and other print materials*
  - ✓ *written mode: provide students information and models of subject-specific language*

THE ROLE OF WRITING

- ◊ Largely unrecognized.
- ◊ Involves decision making at different levels (genre and choices at the level of register).
- ◊ Allows reflection
- ◊ A way of enhancing the learning process due to two kinds of reasons:

**General reasons**

Useful for:

- ✓ Showing what has been learnt.
- ✓ Discovering and knowledge creation.
- ✓ Finding out what students know and don't know.
- ✓ Expanding language resources in the foreign language:
  - Lexical items
  - Grammatical structures
  - Reformulations

Deeper processing of content

**Subject-specific reasons**

Students need help

- ✓ When learning the written register of the subjects (L1 and L2)
- ✓ In the transition from the spoken to the written mode in school subjects

- ✓ Register scaffolding to support students:
  - Macrolevel (planned): sequenced activities, from the spoken mode to the more difficult written mode
  - Microlevel (spontaneous): reformulating the student's spoken production into a more effective and acceptable way

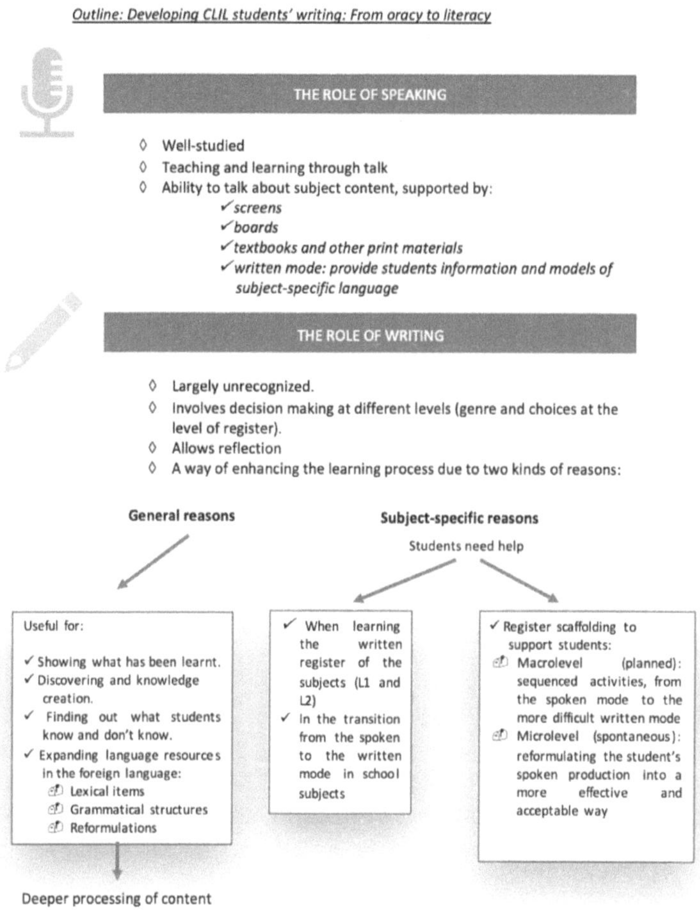

**Figure 2.** Sentence-verbal outline. Source: Own elaboration

## Outline 3. Sentence-visual outline

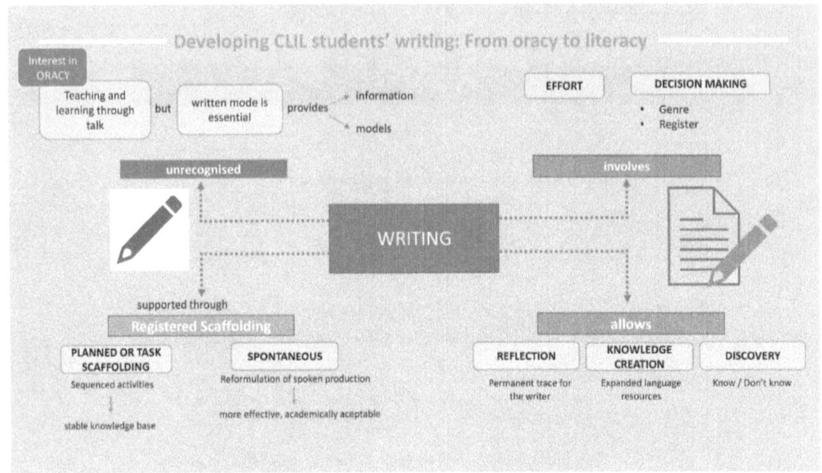


**Figure 3.** Sentence-visual outline. Source: Own elaboration

## Task 6. Checklist phase 3

1. **I know the main types of outlines**
   a. Yes
   b. No
2. **I can differentiate between topic and sentence outlines**
   a. Yes
   b. No
3. **I can distinguish between verbal and visual outlines**
   a. Yes
   b. No
4. **I have found my preferred type of outline**
   a. Yes
   b. No

### *Phase 4: Creating your outline*

The main aim of phase 4 is to create an outline of a text that the learners have already worked with. Students will be able to self-assess their work with the model answer provided. Optionally, they will be able to provide other peers with feedback and receive suggestions from them.

This phase will be developed in 1 hour through three different tasks:

- Task 7 is a production task in which students are required to create their own outline of a text they have already worked with, i.e., a 'summary' outline (writing activity).
- Task 8 is a production task in which they will create their own outline of a different topic, i.e., a 'creative' outline (writing activity).
- Task 9 is a checklist to assess understanding (reading activity).

In task 7, students will choose a text that they have previously worked with in one of their subjects at university. They will decide which type of outline to create, using an app from those presented in the module.

In the second task (task 8), learners are required to create an outline of a topic that they consider interesting, also related to their degrees, but without the support of a text.

Finally, in the assessment task (task 9), students can assess their own learning, checking if they have properly understood the contents of the phase.

### Task 7. Creating your outline

*Now that you have learnt how to make an outline, it is time to create your own. Choose a text that you have previously worked in one of your subjects at university. As you now know several types of outlines (topic outline, sentence-visual outline and sentence-verbal outline), decide which type suits your own needs best. Finally, choose one of apps presented in the introductory video (see app grid), to create your preferred outline.*

## Materials for Task 7. Creating an outline

- **App grid**

| Name of the APP | Purpose | Links |
|---|---|---|
| **Microsoft OneNote** | Sentence and topic outlines | - |
| **Microsoft Word** | Sentence and topic outlines | - |
| **Google Docs** | Sentence and topic outlines | https://docs.google.com/ |
| **CmapTools** | Sentence-visual outlines (mindmaps) | https://cmap.ihmc.us/ |
| **FreeMind** | Sentence-visual outlines (mindmaps) | https://freemind.softonic.com/ |
| **Miro** | Sentence-visual outlines (mindmaps) | http://miro.com |
| **MindMeister** | Sentence-visual outlines (mindmaps) | https://www.mindmeister.com/es |
| **Workflowy** | Topic and sentence-verbal outlines | https://workflowy.com/ |
| **Toodledo** | Topic and sentence-verbal outlines | https://www.toodledo.com/ |
| **Checkvist** | Topic and sentence-verbal outlines | https://checkvist.com/ |
| **Little Outliner** | Topic and sentence-verbal outlines | http://littleoutliner.com/v1/ |
| **Evernote** | Topic and sentence-verbal outlines | https://evernote.com/intl/es |

## Task 8. Creative outline

*Now that you are familiar with how to create outlines from texts, would you like to try something more complex? What happens if there is no initial text?*

*In this task, you are required to create an outline of a topic that you consider interesting. Think about a concept covered in one of your university subjects that is attractive or engaging for you. Gather all the information you can (academic texts, videos, webpages…) to create your outline.*

*You can use one of the apps presented in the 'App grid' (Microsoft OneNote, CmapTools, FreeMind, etc.) to make it more visual.*

*If you cannot think of an attractive topic, check this webpage. Here, you will find several prompts that can give you creative ideas for your outline: https://www.nytimes.com/2018/04/12/learning/over-1000-writing-prompts-for-students.html*

**Task 9. Checklist phase 4**

1. **I am able to create an outline without guidance or support**
   a. Yes
   b. No
2. **I can create different types of outlines**
   a. Yes
   b. No
3. **I can use an app to display my outline**
   a. Yes
   b. No
4. **I can create an outline from a general topic**
   a. Yes
   b. No

Table 6 shows a rubric that has been developed to assess this module and that can be used as a self-assessment, peer-assessment tool for students as well as an evaluation tool for instructors if the module is taught in a class.

*External sources for materials in this module*


- Llinares, A., Morton, T., & Whittaker, R. (2012). Developing CLIL students' writing: From oracy to literacy. In A. Llinares, T. Morton and R. Whittaker, *The Roles of Language in CLIL* (pp. 244–280). Cambridge University Press. Extract reproduced with permission of Cambridge University Press through PLSclear.
- https://www.nytimes.com/2018/04/12/learning/over-1000-writing-prompts-for-students.html

#### 2.2.1.4. Rubric for assessment

**Table 6.** Rubric to assess introductory module 'Creating outlines'

| Element | Excellent (4) | Good (3) | Fair (2) | Poor (1) |
|---|---|---|---|---|
| **Content Elements** | | | | |
| Ideas from original text (for 'summary' outlines) | All the ideas from the original text are included. | Most of the ideas from the original text are included. | Some ideas from the original text are included. | Only focuses on one idea from the original text. |
| Outline hierarchy | Includes main ideas, supporting ideas and details. | Includes main ideas and supporting ideas. | Includes only the main ideas of the text. | Mixes ideas without distinguishing between main and supporting ideas. |
| Type of outlines proposed | Chooses a type of outline in which the information is clear and organised, with cohesion and coherence. | Mixes different types of outlines, but the information is clearly organised. | The content of the outline is displayed in a disorganised way, but it can be understood. | There is no organisation, cohesion or coherence among the ideas of the outline. |
| **Language Elements** | | | | |
| Paraphrasing the source text (for 'summary' outlines) | Does not include sentences directly copied from the original text and uses connectors. | There are hardly any sentences copied from the text, but these are correctly referenced. | Copies a couple of literal sentences from the original text without referencing the author. | Most of the outline is comprised of copied sentences from the author. |
| Inclusion of formal elements (passive voice, nominalisations, etc.) | A wide variety of formal elements are included. | Sufficient formal elements are included. | Some formal elements are included. | Formal elements scarcely appear/ no formal elements are used. |

### *2.2.2. Module 1: Concept maps*

#### **2.2.2.1. Overview and aims**

This module aims to provide students with the fundamental knowledge and tools to create concept maps. This topic will be introduced over four different self-study, online task phases, implementing both theoretical aspects and practical exercises under the principles of self-study and self-assessment.

Concept maps make learning contents more visible. They are particularly helpful for visual learners, but any type of learner can benefit from them. Concept maps are a very useful tool for developing a logical structure to organise and represent information visually. They can help learners to see the big picture of the contents they are dealing with. Concept mapping is a powerful strategy that helps learners identify relationships between ideas and concepts and visualise the structure of the information they are dealing with, so it will be useful for clarifying and structuring ideas and recalling the information. Finally, they can be very helpful when expanding an outline (introductory module), for writing summaries (module 3) and for creating presentations (module 5). You can check the modules on these topics for further information.

The interactive version of the module developed in *Genial.ly* can be accessed here: https://view.genial.ly/6040aa0545e4040d2f09f9c9/learning-experience-didactic-unit-concept-maps-moduleicluex
And the introductory video hosted in the *L2EARN* channel in YouTube is also freely available: https://www.youtube.com/watch?v=HExi8WXtQd8
At the end of this module students will be able to:

- Create their own concept map on a given topic without any type of guidance or support.
- Build a concept map including the main elements and characteristics of concept mapping in their productions: concepts, linking words, propositions, and the hierarchical structure of downward arrows and cross-links by using the concept mapping software *CmapTools* or a similar type of programme.
- Self-assess their own performance.

In addition, students will be able to understand written and oral input, as well as to produce written output related to the content objective. They will also be able to expand their knowledge and use of 'concepts' (concrete/abstract nouns) and 'linking words/phrases' (conjunctions and connectors) in context.

The module is designed to be completed in 3 hours, so students' workload should not be longer than this. According to the Common European Framework of Reference (CEFR), it is adapted to B2 level (English), and will contribute to the development of the following skills: Spoken comprehension and written comprehension.

#### 2.2.2.2. Learning outcomes

The *language skills (CEFR)* that are going to be dealt with in this module are the following:

1. Comprehension:
   (a) Written:
      - Can scan quickly through long and complex texts, locating relevant details.
      - Can obtain information, ideas and opinions from highly specialised sources within his/her field.
      - Can recognise when a text provides factual information and when it seeks to convince readers of something.
      - Can recognise different structures in discursive text: contrasting arguments, problem-solution presentation and cause-effect relationships.

   (b) Spoken:
      - Can understand the main ideas of propositionally and linguistically complex speech on both concrete and abstract topics delivered in standard speech, including technical discussions in his/her field of specialization.
      - Can follow extended speech and complex lines of argument provided the topic is reasonably familiar, and the direction of the talk is sign-posted by explicit markers.

- Can understand recordings in the standard form of the language likely to be encountered in social, professional, or academic life and identify speaker viewpoints and attitudes as well as the information content.

In this module, students will also work on some *functions*:

- Comparing
- Contrasting

And the *language foci* will be:

- To use prefixes and suffixes to form new meaningful words in context.
- To understand static and dynamic linking words/phrases forming propositions in context.
- To become familiar with different types of linking words/phrases in English.
- To assess the accurate use of linking words/phrases in context.
- To be able to use linking words/phrases in context.

#### 2.2.2.3. Contents: Phases and tasks

Table 7 shows the activities that are going to be carried out in the module.

**Table 7.** List of activities for module 1 'Concept maps'

| Phase | Aim | Tasks | Description | Time | Typology |
|---|---|---|---|---|---|
| Phase 1 | To introduce what concept maps are and how they work. | Task 1: video & questionnaire | *Presentation task*: First contact with concept maps. | 15' | Reading Listening |
| | | Task 2: checklist | *Assessment task*: perception checklist. | 5' | Reading |
| Phase 2 | To present concept mapping: the main elements and characteristics of concept maps: concepts, linking words/ phrases,propositions, crosslinks and the structure/ organisation of concept maps with real samples. | Task 3: what are concept maps? | *Presentation task*: Introduction to the main elements and characteristics of concept maps. | 10' | Listening |
| | | Task 4: identifying features of concept maps | *Practice task*: Identifying concepts, linking words, propositions and cross-links. | 15' | Reading |
| | | Task 5: checklist | *Assessment task*: perception checklist. | 5' | Reading |
| Phase 3 | To practise the use of concepts and linking words/ phrases in concept mappings. | Task 6: completing a concept map from a text | *Presentation task*: Reading of a text in order to complete a concept map with the information about this text. | 5' | Reading |
| | | Task 7: completing Concept Maps | *Practice task*: fill-the-gap practice of concepts and linking words to complete a concept map. | 15' | Reading |
| | | Task 8: Cmapping concept maps | *Production task*: creation of concept maps with *CmapTools* on the computer. | 25' | Language focus |
| | | Task 9: looking up concepts | *Extension task – concepts*: extension of knowledge on what concepts are, from a linguistic point of view. | 20' | Language focus |
| | | Task 10: building concept maps | *Extension task – linking words:* extension of knowledge on the types of linking words/phrases that can be found, from a linguistic point of view. | 20' | Language focus |
| | | Task 11: checklist | *Assessment task*: perception checklist. | 5' | Reading |

**Table 7.** Continued

| Phase | Aim | Tasks | Description | Time | Typology |
|---|---|---|---|---|---|
| Phase 4 | To assess students' building of their own concept map with *CmapTools* but without any other type of support. | Task 12: creating a concept map from a video | *Presentation task*: watching a video to create student's own concept map from it. | 5' | Listening |
| | | Task 13: creating your own concept map | *Production task*: Creation of a concept map including the main elements and characteristics of concept mapping with *CmapTools* (without any type of guidance or support). | 20' | Language Focus |
| | | Task 14: assessing concept maps | *Assessment task*: peer-assessment providing feedback on peers' concept maps creations. | 10' | Reading |
| | | Task 15: checklist | *Assessment task:* perception checklist. | 5' | Reading |

### *Phase 1: Warm-up*

The main teaching objective of this phase is for students to become familiar with concept maps, and with how concept mapping works as a knowledge representation tool.

Phase 1 will be completed in 20 minutes through two different tasks:

- Task 1 is a presentation task to test previous knowledge about concept maps and to present the basic notions about concept maps (reading and listening activity).
- Task 2 is a checklist to assess understanding (reading activity).

In the presentation task (task 1), students will be asked to complete the six-question questionnaire on concept maps after watching the introductory video about concept maps: https://youtu.be/HExi8WXtQd8 and looking at Figure 4

In the assessment task (task 2), students will assess their own learning.

**Task 1. Questionnaire on concept maps.**

1. **What is a 'concept map'?**
   a. A diagram with line drawing / a line-drawing diagramme comprised of symbols representing key objects and actions that occur within a system.
   b. A picture or word placed in the middle of the page, with several 'legs' which are drawn radiating outwards.
   c. A type of graph in which a circle is divided into sectors with each of them representing a part of the whole.
   d. A hierarchy of concepts, usually drawn within circles or boxes, and relationships between them, which are indicated by lines drawn to show their connection.
2. **How would you define 'concept'?**
   a. A regularity or pattern in events or objects, or records of events or objects, designated by a label (Novak, 1984).
   b. A group of statements joined by linking words.
   c. A statement about any objects or events in the universe. It contains two or more concepts connected using linking words.
   d. None of the above are right answers.
3. **Concept maps have specific characteristics that distinguish them from other knowledge representation tools. One of their characteristics is:**
   a. Concept maps tend to be read from top to bottom.
   b. Concept maps tend to be read from bottom to top.
   c. On a concept map, each concept consists of the maximum number of words needed to depict the object or event.
   d. Concept maps implicitly express the most relevant relationships between a set of concepts.
4. **In Figure 4, observe how the concept "amphibians" is linked to the concept "lungs", each of which are joined in the same subdomain of the concept map by the linking word "have". What do "linking words" refer to?**

a. They are the set of words used to link concepts in order to express the static relationships between the concepts in a concept map.
b. They are the set of statements used to express dynamic relations between concepts.
c. They are the set of words used to join concepts to express static or dynamic relationships between (usually) two concepts.
d. They are the group of statements which express the relationship that exists between the joined concepts.

5. **In Figure 4, the linking word "reproduce" joins the concept "amphibians" with the concept "sexually", forming the proposition "amphibians reproduce sexually". What is a proposition?**
   a. A set of two concepts joined by static linking words.
   b. A group of two or more statements joined by static or dynamic linking words.
   c. A meaningful statement containing two or more concepts connected by linking words or phrases.
   d. A group of words containing two or more concepts joined by linking words to form meaningless statements.
6. **In Figure 4, observe how the concept "in water" is linked to the concept "gills", both of which are in separate subdomains of the concept map, forming cross-links. What does cross-link mean?**
   a. Cross-links help us see relationships from top to bottom and from bottom to top.
   b. Cross-links help us see how a concept in one domain of knowledge represented on the map is related to a concept in another domain shown on the map.
   c. Cross-links help us see cause-consequence relationships.
   d. Cross-links help us express explicitly the most relevant relationships among a set of concepts.

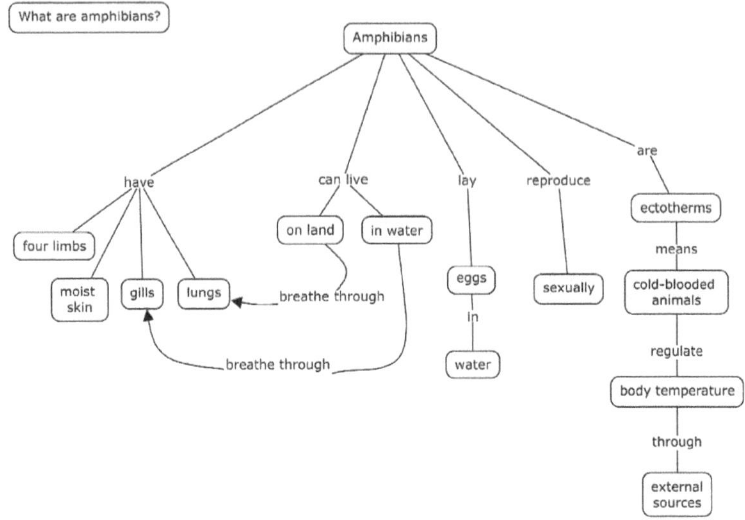


**Figure 4.** Concept map about 'Amphibians'. Source: Own elaboration

## Task 2. Checklist phase 1

1. **I have completed task 1 ('Test Yourself! How much do you know about 'concept maps'?')**
   a. Yes
   b. No
2. **I have answered correctly all the questions in the prior-knowledge questionnaire.**
   a. Yes
   b. No
3. **I understand what a 'concept map' is.**
   a. Yes
   b. No
4. **I know which specific characteristics distinguish 'concept maps' from other representation tools.**
   a. Yes
   b. No

5. **I have learned about the origins of concept mapping.**
   a. Yes
   b. No

### *Phase 2: Pre-task phase*

The main aim of this phase is to identify the main elements and characteristics of concept maps: concepts, linking words/phrases, and the structure/organization of concept maps in real samples.

It will be completed in 30 minutes through three different tasks:

- Task 3 is a presentation task where students will learn what a concept map is.
- Task 4 is a practice task where the main features of concept maps are identified.
- Task 5 is a checklist to assess understanding.

In task 3, students are asked to watch again the introductory video paying special attention to the main elements and characteristics of concept mapping: concepts, linking words, propositions, cross-links, and the structure of concept maps.

Task 4 is a practice task in which students are required to identify the elements and characteristics of concept mapping in a concept map using *CmapTools*. First, students must pay attention to how the different elements and characteristics of concept mapping are highlighted in the identified concept map entitled 'Sun' (Figure 6) from an unidentified concept map (Figure 5). After that, students will identify the same elements and characteristics but this time in an unidentified concept map on a different topic, i.e., 'Amphibians' (Figure 4). Students are asked to identify and distinguish between concepts, linking words/phrases, propositions, crosslinks and the structure/organisation of concept maps in real samples.

Finally, in the assessment task (task 5), students can assess their own learning by checking if they have understood the contents of this phase.

## Task 3. What are concept maps?

*Watch again the introductory video available at: https://youtu.be/HExi 8WXtQd8.*

*Pay attention to the main elements and characteristics of concept mapping: concepts, linking words, propositions, cross-links, and the structure of concept maps.*

## Task 4. Identifying the features of concept maps.

*First, look at the sample concept map entitled 'Sun' (Figure 6) and compare it with the same, unidentified concept map (Figure 5). You must pay attention to how the elements and characteristics of concept mapping are highlighted using different formats (identified concept map):*

- *Concepts: in capital letters and grouped as abstract nouns (square-shaped) and concrete nouns (circle-shaped).*
- *Linking words/phrases: written in small-case and grouped into dynamic (non-bold font) and static (bold font).*
- *Organisation/structure:*
  - *Propositions: surrounded by downward, straight lines.*
  - *Cross-links: surrounded by curved arrows.*

*Now, identify the same elements and characteristics of concept mapping you found in the previous concept map but this time in a different concept map entitled 'Amphibians' (Figure 4). Identify 'concepts', 'linking words/phrases', as well as the 'organisation/structure' of the concept map. Use CmapTools to create the same concept map 'Amphibians' on your computer. Please, follow the instructions below and highlight the elements and characteristics of the unidentified concept map 'Birds' (Figure 4). Once you have finished, you may check your answers with the ones provided in figure 19 in the answer key.*

## Materials for Task 4. 'Identifying the features of concept maps'

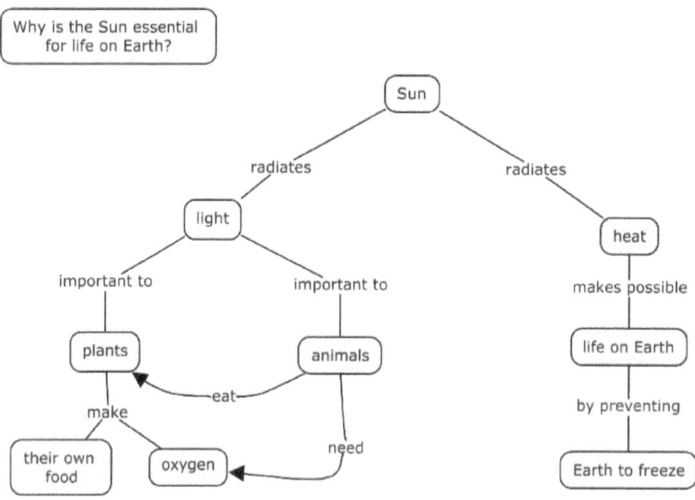


**Figure 5.** Unidentified concept map 'Sun'. Source: Own elaboration

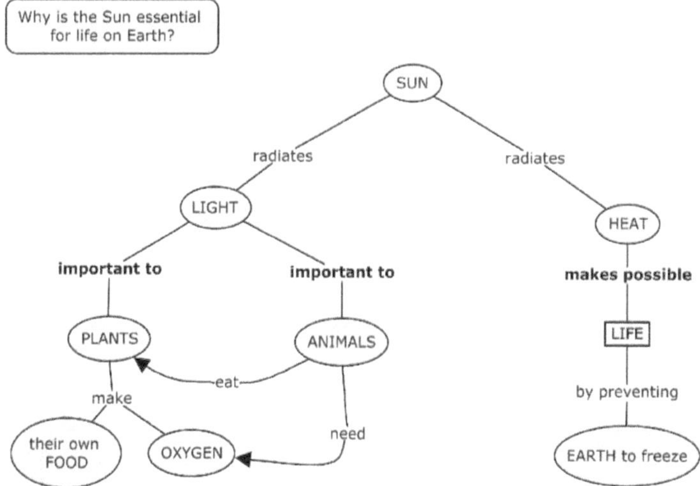


**Figure 6.** Identified concept map about the 'Sun'. Source: Own elaboration

**Task 5. Checklist phase 2**

1. **I have watched the video "Concept mapping".**
   a. Yes
   b. No
2. **I can identify the concrete and abstract concepts in the concept map.**
   a. Yes
   b. No
3. **I can identify all the linking words and phrases in the concept map.**
   a. Yes
   b. No
4. **I can identify the organisation / structure in the concept map.**
   a. Yes
   b. No
5. **I have completed the whole task with *CmapTools*.**
   a. Yes
   b. No

### *Phase 3: Task phase*

The main teaching objective of this phase is to use concepts and linking words/phrases in real concept maps.

The duration of this phase will vary between 50 and 90 minutes and will be include six tasks:

- Task 6 is a presentation task to understand the text provided (reading activity).
- Task 7 is a practice task to complete an unfinished concept map (reading activity).
- Task 8 is a production task to use *CmapTools* (language focus activity).
- Task 9 is an extension, optional task to learn about the linguistic aspects of concepts and word formation (language focus activity).

- Task 10 is an extension task to learn about different types of linking words/phrases (language focus activity).
- Task 11 is a checklist to assess understanding (reading activity).

In the presentation task (task 6), students will be asked to read the text 'Preventing infections' (Text 1 below). They will need to understand what the text is about in order to complete a concept map with the information about this text. To fulfil this task, students will be provided with a concept map on text 1 to be partially completed (Figure 7).

In task 7, students will complete the given unfinished concept map in which some 'concepts' and 'linking words/phrases' are missing (Figure 7). Students will fill in the gaps with the correct 'concepts' and 'linking words/phrases' from the boxes below the concept map. After finishing the task, students can check the model answer (figure 20) in the answer key.

In task 8, students will create the same concept map from the previous task on their computers, using *CmapTools*, so it will be necessary for them to access this online tool, which is available at https://cmap.ihmc.us/.

The extension task (task 9) is optional. Students will work on how concepts are defined, from a linguistic point of view. First, they will look up certain concepts in an online dictionary in order to practice the linguistic difference between 'concrete' and 'abstract' nouns.

Additionally, with the help of a dictionary, students will practice word formation of the concepts presented while completing a table with the corresponding noun/verb/adjective/adverb in each gap where necessary. Finally, students will be asked to complete sentences using the word in capitals to form a new word that fits in the gap.

Task 10 is also an extension task in which students will work on different types of linking words/phrases from a linguistic perspective. First, students are asked to match linking words/phrases with the corresponding type. Students will also practice their knowledge of linking words/phrases by spotting the odd one out. At the end of the task, students will complete propositions with one of the linking words/phrases provided.

Finally, in the assessment task (task 11), students can assess their own learning, checking if they have understood the contents of the phase.

## Task 6. Completing a concept map from a text

Materials for Task 6. 'Completing a concept map from a text'

### Text 1: 'Preventing infections'

*An infection is an illness caused by microscopic organisms (bacteria, fungi, parasites or viruses) that enter our body and affect its functions. These organisms are known as pathogens. To avoid infections and protect ourselves and others, we need to block pathogens from entering our body. How can we do this? There are two main possibilities: natural and artificial barriers.*

*Natural barriers*

*Natural barriers are lines of defence that the human body has to block pathogens from entering our body. They are:*

1. *The skin that covers our body's surface. It protects us from invasive pathogens.*
2. *Mucous membranes that lubricate and protect organs. They are coated with secretions such as mucus, saliva, tears or gastric juices in the stomach that fight microorganisms.*

*Artificial barriers*

*Artificial barriers are man-made products (like gloves or condoms) and specific techniques (such as disinfection and sterilisation) that reduce the risk of infection and are particularly important in health-care settings (e.g., hospitals). They are contamination-control techniques.*

1. *Disinfection (also known as antiseptic) techniques allow germ reduction. Disease-causing microorganisms are reduced in number or inactivated. It is a mandatory procedure in health-care settings and in the food industry. Disinfection techniques can be applied to non-living objects (for example, when bleach is used) or to living tissue (e.g., on the skin or mucous membranes) by means of chemical substances such as ethanol or iodine.*
2. *Sterilisation (or aseptic) techniques are used to kill harmful pathogens (including bacteria, viruses and bacterial spores). The basic techniques of sterilisation are physical (through the use of heat) or chemical (by means of certain substances such as formaldehyde or ethylene oxide).*

Source: Own elaboration

## Task 7. Completing concept maps

| Materials for Task 7. 'Completing concept maps' |
|---|

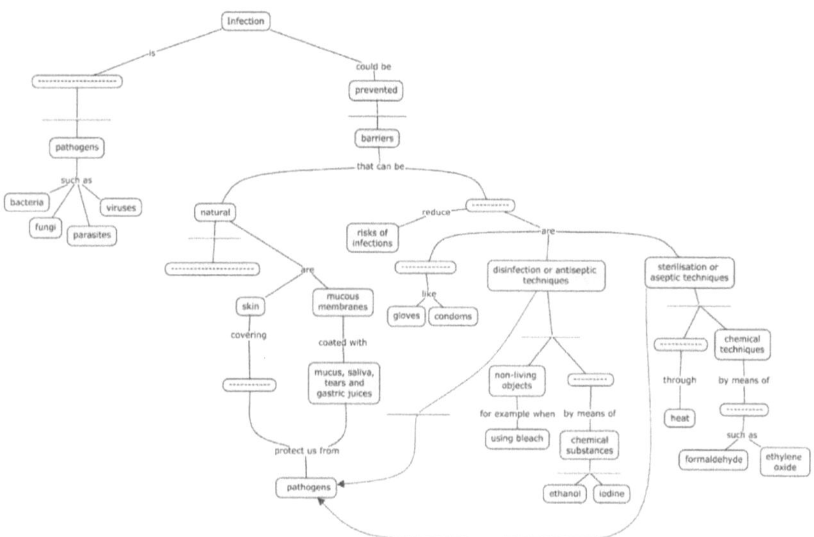


**Figure 7.** Concept map 'Preventing infections'. Source: Own elaboration

| **Concepts** | | | |
|---|---|---|---|
| 1. living tissue | 2. artificial | 3. substances | 4. an illness caused by microscopic organisms |
| 5. our body's surface | 6. physical techniques | 7. man-made products | 8. lines of defence that our body has |

| **Linking words/phrases** | | | |
|---|---|---|---|
| 1. also known as | 2. can be applied to | 3. through | 4. such as |
| 5. kill | 6. reduce or inactivate | 7. include | 8. defined as |

## Task 8. Cmapping concept maps

*Now, you are ready to create a digital version of your concept map using CmapTools, which is available at https://cmap.ihmc.us/. You just need to follow the instructions provided.*

## Task 9. Looking up concepts

### Activity 1

*Look up the following nouns in a dictionary (e.g., www.macmillandictionary.com): (1) substance; (2) infection; (3) germ; (4) organism; (5) technique; (6) sterilization; (7) secretion; (8) effect; (9) disinfection; (10) mechanism.*

*Write the meanings of the words according to the context of the text, and group them into 'concrete' and 'abstract'. The first one is done for you as an example.*

### Activity 2

*With the help of a dictionary, complete the table in Activity 2, writing the corresponding noun/verb/adjective/adverb in each gap where necessary. In some cases, you have suffixes and prefixes to help you create the new forms of the words. Remember that words are formed by adding prefixes and/or suffixes to a root. Sometimes they do not share the same meaning, but they share the same roots.*

## Activity 3

*Complete the sentences using the word in bold to form a new word that fits in the gap. The first one is done for you as an example.*

| Materials for Task 9. 'Looking up concepts' |
|---|

| **Activity 1.** |
|---|

| 1. substance | 2. infection | 3. germ | 4. organism | 5. technique |
|---|---|---|---|---|
| 6. sterilization | 7. secretion | 8. effect | 9. disinfection | 10. mechanism |

**Example:**

1. **substance: a particular type of liquid, solid, or gas.**
2. infection:
3. germ:
4. organism:
5. technique:
6. secretion:
7. effect:
8. mechanism:

| **Concrete nouns** | **Abstract nouns** |
|---|---|
| | |

## Activity 2.

| Word formation | | | |
|---|---|---|---|
| **Noun** | **Verb** | **Adjective** | **Adverb** |
| Substance | X | Substan**tial** | Substantial**ly** |
| Infection | ______ | **-ous**<br>**-ed**<br>**-ive** | X |
| Germ<br>**-ation** | **-ate** | X | X |
| Organism<br>____ | **-ise/-ize** | **-ic** (x2) | X |
| Technique<br>**-ian** | X | **-al** | **-ly** |
| Secretion | ______ | **-ive** | **-ly** |
| Effect | ______ | **-ive**<br>**in- + -ive** | **-ly**<br>**in- + -ly** |
| Mechanism | X | **-al** | **-ly** |

## Activity 3.

*Example: The study shows very _____**substantial**_____ differences between population groups.*

***SUBSTANCE***

1. He's very __________ about his past in Scotland. **SECRETION**
2. If you come back to school too soon, you might __________ other people. **INFECTION**
3. He's the most __________ skilled player in the team. **TECHNIQUE**
4. It's been freezing cold for seeds to __________ properly. **GERM**
5. The National Health Service has a register of potential __________ donors. **ORGANISM**
6. The factory has shut down due to __________ problems. **MECHANISM**
7. Unfortunately, the new policy has been __________ in cutting crime. **EFFECT**

## Task 10. Building concept maps.

### Activity 1

*Look at the linking words/phrases listed and match each box containing the linking words/phrases with the corresponding label.*

### Activity 2

*Circle the linking word/phrase that is the odd one out in each case. The first one is done for you as an example.*

### Activity 3

*Complete the propositions with one of the linking words/phrases provided. Use only one word to fill each gap. The first one is done for you as an example.*

| Materials for task 10. 'Building concept maps' |
|---|

| **Activity 1.** |
|---|

a. contrast (differences)
b. contrast (similarities)
c. giving examples
d. reasons & causes
e. results & consequences
f. showing purpose

| |
|---|
| for example<br>for instance<br>including<br>such as<br>to illustrate |

| |
|---|
| with the intention of<br>so that<br>in order (not) to |

| |
|---|
| due to<br>because of<br>owing to<br>thanks to<br>caused by<br>following<br>on account of<br>that is why |

| |
|---|
| as a result of<br>as a consequence of |

| |
|---|
| as opposed to<br>instead of<br>in comparison with<br>even though<br>but<br>yet<br>although<br>in spite of<br>whereas<br>while |

| |
|---|
| similar to<br>in the same way as |

**Activity 2.**

*Example: thanks to / due to /* so that

1. such as / following / for instance
2. as a result of / as a consequence of / owing to
3. yet / similar to / as opposed to
4. including / with the intention of / in order to

**Activity 3.**

*Example: She almost died* __ due / owing __ *to food poisoning.*

1. I am keen on extreme sports __________ as surfing, rallycross, and canyoning.
2. Regular controls are required with the __________ of preventing a new outbreak of coronavirus.
3. They have decided to move to their village as a __________ of the ongoing protests and riots.
4. The pandemic situation across Spain is __________ to what Italy is going through at the moment.
5. Flights prices will rise over the summer __________ of keeping regular fares.

## Task 11. Checklist phase 3

1. **I have read the text 'How to avoid infections' before completing the concept map with the correct 'concepts' or 'linking words/phrases'.**
   a. Yes
   b. No
2. **I have filled in all the gaps in the concept map with the correct 'concepts' and 'linking words/phrases'.**
   a. Yes
   b. No
3. **I know that 'concepts' are depicted within circles/boxes in the concept map.**
   a. Yes
   b. No

4. **I know that 'linking words/phrases' are located on the lines connecting 'concepts' in the concept map.**
   a. Yes
   b. No
5. **I have used *CmapTools*.**
   a. Yes
   b. No

### *Phase 4: Follow-up phase*

The main learning objective of this phase is to create a concept map including the main elements and characteristics of concept mapping with *CmapTools* (without any type of guidance or support).

Phase 4 will be completed in 30–40 minutes through 4 tasks:

- Task 12 is a presentation task in which students watch a video and then, create a concept map (listening activity).
- Task 13 is a practice task to create their own concept map (reading activity).
- Task 14 is an assessment task to check their partners' concept maps (reading activity).
- Task 15 is presented as a checklist to assess understanding (reading activity).

In the presentation task (task 12), students are asked to watch the video 'What is a coronavirus?' by Elizabeth Cox to create their own concept map from it. The video is available at: https://www.youtube.com/watch?v=D9tTi-CDjDU&ab_channel=TED-Ed.

In practice task 13, students will use *CmapTools* to create their own concept map, without any type of support, on their computers based on the information found in the video proposed in the previous task. They are provided with a model answer to check that they have included all the required elements (Figure 8).

Task 14 is a collaborative task in which students will need to find a partner and check their concept map on the video 'What is a coronavirus'. The instructor can decide how many concept maps must be assessed by each student. Students will follow the assessment criteria from the rubric 'Peer-assessment rubric on concept maps' (Table 8).

Finally, in the last assessment task (task 15), students can assess their own learning, checking if they have understood the contents of the phase.

**Task 13. Creating your own concept map.**

**Activity 1**

*Use CmapTools to create your own concept map on your computers. Remember that your concept map must include all the elements and characteristics of concept maps:*

- *Concrete and abstract concepts*
- *Static and dynamic linking words/phrases*
- *Static and dynamic propositions*
- *Hierarchical structure with downward arrows and cross-links.*

**Activity 2**

*Compare your own concept map with the sample provided in the answer key (Figure 21) to check that you have included all the elements.*

**Task 14. Scanning concept maps.**

**Activity 1**

*Check your partner's/partners' concept map on the video 'What is a coronavirus?' (Elizabeth Cox) following the assessment criteria from the rubric (Table 8) to support your feedback.*

## Material for Task 14. 'Assessing concept maps'

**Table 8.** Peer-assessment rubric on 'Concept maps'*

| Criteria | Levels (mark with a cross how s/he has done it) | | Suggestions (explain or illustrate how you would do it) |
|---|---|---|---|
| 1. Concepts | 1. In most cases, the selected concepts do not refer to groupings of objects or events in the same category, so there are many extra or missing concepts. | | |
| | 2. Although the selected concepts mostly refer to objects and events in the same category, they are not well defined or formulated. | | |
| | 3. The selected concepts mostly refer to objects and events in the same category. They are well formulated, but they are all concrete concepts (lacking any level of abstraction). | | |
| | 4. The selected concepts mostly refer to objects and events in the same category. They are well formulated and both concrete and abstract notions are used. | | |
| 2. Linking words | 1. Either all or most of the linking words are missing, or most of the selected words do not represent explicit links between concepts. | | |
| | 2. For the most part, there are suitable linking words to relate concepts, but linking words and concepts are mixed up in some cases. | | |
| | 3. Linking words are used to connect all the concepts and they clearly and explicitly represent the relationships between them. However, they are all within the same category: they establish either dynamic or static relationships. | | |
| | 4. Linking words are used to connect all concepts and they clearly and explicitly represent the relationship between them, establishing both dynamic and static relationships. | | |

* I would like to thank Dr. Manuel Lucero Fustes from the department of Educational Sciences at the University of Extremadura for his invaluable help in designing this rubric.

**Table 8.** Continued

| **Criteria** | **Levels (mark with a cross how s/he has done it)** | | **Suggestions (explain or illustrate how you would do it)** |
|---|---|---|---|
| 3. Propositions | 1. None of the propositions made up by the concepts and the linking words can be read or understood independently (they do not convey any meaning). | | |
| | 2. Most of the propositions made up by the concepts and the linking words can be read or understood independently. However, all the propositions presented by the student are static. | | |
| | 3. All the propositions made up by the concepts and the linking words can be read or understood independently. However, all these propositions are static. | | |
| | 4. All the propositions made up by the concepts and the linking words can be read or understood independently, and they include static and dynamic propositions. | | |
| 4. Organization | 1. The concept map does not have a clear hierarchical structure. It does not start from general, inclusive concepts positioned at the top with more specific concepts arranged hierarchically below (following a typical top to bottom structure). | | |
| | 2. The concept map has more than one structure (cyclical, spidergram, flow, etc.). These structures are not consistently established as different types of lines are used that do not coherently illustrate the relationships between the concepts. | | |
| | 3. The concept map has a hierarchical structure, the concepts being arranged from the most general to the most specific, and only well-differentiated hierarchical relationships (solid lines without arrows) established between the concepts. | | |
| | 4. The concept map has a clear hierarchical structure. The concepts are arranged from the most general to the most specific, and coordination relationships are also established between the concepts from different "branches". | | |

**i** Concept maps are graphic tools used for organizing and representing knowledge. They include three key components: "concepts", "linking words" and "propositions".

(*Continued*)

**Table 8.** Continued

**ii** Novak & Gowin (1984) defines a "concept" as a perceived regularity or pattern in events or objects, or records of event or objects, designated by a label. Flavel, Miller, and Miller (2002) roughly define a concept as a mental grouping of different entities into a single category based on some underlying similarity, some way in which all entities are alike, or some common core that makes them all, in a certain way, the same thing.

**iii** Concepts can be objects and events. Both objects and events are necessary to represent knowledge. The term "events" includes changes of state. For example, "increase in the quality of education" is a concept that is an event, in the same way as the "adoption of constructivism" and the "growth of plants". An examination of a large number of concept maps has shown that most of them have to do primarily with objects, not with events (Safayeni et al., 2005). Using concepts that are events leads to more explanatory concept maps, whereas employing concepts that are objects leads to more descriptive and often rather classifying concept maps.

**iv** Linking words or linking phrases are the set of words used to link ideas in order to express the relationship between (usually) two concepts.

**v** Propositions are sentences about some object or event in the universe (a concept), be it either natural or man-made. They contain two or more concepts connected by linking words or phrases in order to form a meaningful statement.

**vi** Static relations lead to static propositions, while dynamic relations produce dynamic propositions. In general, the adequate representation of knowledge requires both static and dynamic propositions, since the latter captures covariation and the changing relationships between two or more concepts (Derbentseva, Safayeni, & Cañas 2004).

**vii** Concept maps tend to be hierarchical, with the most general concepts at the top and the most specific at the bottom. However, this hierarchical character does not necessarily imply a hierarchical physical structure, as concept maps can also be cyclical (Safayeni et al., 2005) or have more than one root concept. Actually, it is much easier to start by building hierarchical concept maps with a single root concept.

**viii** For hierarchical relationships (from the most general to the most specific concepts), CmapTools recommends using exclusively solid lines without arrows. Regarding coordination relationships (between different concepts belonging to different "branches"), it is recommended to use continuous lines with arrows.

## Task 15. Checklist phase 4.

1. **I have watched the video 'What is a Coronavirus?' (Elizabeth Cox) in order to understand the information needed to create my own concept map.**
   a. Yes
   b. No

2. **I have created my own concept map on the video 'What is a Coronavirus?' (Elizabeth Cox) with *Cmaptools*.**
   a. Yes
   b. No
3. **I have included the elements and characteristics of concept maps: concepts; linking words/phrases; propositions; and the hierarchical structure with downward arrows and cross-links.**
   a. Yes
   b. No
4. **I have compared my own concept map with the sample concept map given on 'What is a Coronavirus?' (Elizabeth Cox).**
   a. Yes
   b. No
5. **I have provided any of my partner/partners with feedback on their building of their concept map in the forum.**
   a. Yes
   b. No

Table 9 shows a rubric that has been developed to assess this module and that can be used as a self-assessment, peer-assessment tool for students as well as an evaluation tool for instructors if the module is taught in a class.

*External sources for materials in this module*

- *CmapTools:* https://cmap.ihmc.us/docs/concept.php
- TED Talk by Elizabeth Cox 'What is a coronavirus?'. Available at https://youtu.be/D9tTi-CDjDU

### 2.2.2.4. Rubric for assessment

**Table 9.** Rubric to assess module 1 'Concept maps'

| **Element** | **Excellent (4)** | **Good (3)** | **Fair (2)** | **Poor (1)** |
|---|---|---|---|---|
| **Content Elements** | | | | |
| Elements and organisation of the concept map | It includes all the required elements: concepts, linking words, propositions, cross-links and focus question. Uses a hierarchical structure. | It includes all the required elements (concepts, linking words, propositions, cross-links and focus question) but the structure could be better organised. | It includes only some of the required elements and the structure is not very clear. | Most of the required elements of a concept map are missing and the structure is not clear. |
| **Language Elements** | | | | |
| Synthesis of information | The information is synthesised, clearly linked, and reflects the main points of the initial text. | The information is not cohesively synthesised. The relations between concepts could be more precise. | The information is poorly synthesised, only the main points of the text are reflected in the concept map. Links are overlooked. | The information is not synthesised, nor it is coherently linked. |
| Linking words | A wide variety of linking words are included: to provide examples, reasons and causes, results and consequences, to show purpose and to establish contrast. | Sufficient linking words are included, although only some of the functions are presented. | Some linking words are included. | Few or no linking words are used. |
| **Extra-Elements** | **Yes (4)** | | **No (1)** | |
| Use of online tools | Some of the online tools included in the module have been used. | | Online tools have not been employed. | |

### *2.2.3. Module 2: Writing definitions*

#### 2.2.3.1. Overview and aims

This module aims to provide students with the fundamental knowledge and tools to write definitions. This topic will be introduced through five different self-study phases, implementing both theoretical aspects and practical exercises under the principles of self-study and self-assessment. In short, the goal of this module is to provide the knowledge necessary to understand and write definitions.

Definitions are defined by Llinares et al. (2012) as a 'mini-genre', often part of descriptive reports. They state that definitions are very common in CLIL secondary school classes and that teachers attach great importance to this academic function. Students are expected to understand the definitions provided by experts in the materials used in the classroom and produce their own definitions that will become more complex as they progress through school. University students are also expected to become familiar with the terminology of their field of expertise and understanding and producing complex definitions is also very important at this more advanced stage. In fact, in their book on academic writing aimed at graduate students, Swales and Feak (2012) devote a section to definitions and suggest that one of the situations in which university students should offer a definition of a term would be when they need to display their understanding for a course paper or examination. They also argue that textbooks include definitions to clarify terms that the reader may not be familiar with, but sometimes students at university are also expected to demonstrate their understanding of specific concepts with personal, complex definitions.

The interactive version of the module developed in *Genial.ly* can be accessed here: https://view.genial.ly/60467d4030d8a70d14c69f87/learning-experience-didactic-unit-writing-definitionsmodule
And the introductory video hosted in our *L2EARN* channel in YouTube is also freely available: https://www.youtube.com/watch?v=I2S1spAdMk4&t=2s
At the end of this module, students will be able to:

- Create their own glossary of the terms of the module.
- Understand definitions and become familiar with the language used in them.

- Use the correct language structures to write an adequate definition.
- Self-assess their own performance at the end of each phase.

Students will also be able to understand written input as well as produce written output related to the content objectives.

The module is designed to be completed in 6 hours, so the student workload should not be longer than this. According to the Common European Framework of Reference (CEFR), it is adapted to B2 level (English), and will contribute to the development of the following skills: spoken comprehension, written comprehension and written production.

### 2.2.3.2. Learning outcomes

The *language skills (CEFR)* that are going to be dealt with in this module are the following:

1. Comprehension:
   (a) Written:
   - Can scan quickly through long and complex texts, locating relevant details.

   (b) Spoken:
   - Can understand recordings in the standard form of the language likely to be encountered in social, professional or academic life and identify speaker viewpoints and attitudes as well as the information content.

2. Production:
   (a) Written:
   - Can write a detailed description of a complex process.
   - Can write clear, detailed descriptions of real or imaginary events and experiences marking the relationship between ideas in clear connected text and following established conventions of the genre concerned.

Some other *functions* will also be dealt with in this module:

- Identifying key ideas.
- Organising information.
- Defining terms.

And the main *language focus* is:

– Defining verbs

### 2.2.3.3. Contents: Phases and tasks

The activities that are going to be carried out in this module are shown in Table 10 below

## Table 10. List of activities for module 2 'Writing definitions'

**Table 10.** List of activities for module 2 'Writing definitions'

| Phase | Aim | Tasks | Description | Time | Typology |
|---|---|---|---|---|---|
| Phase 1 | To introduce what a definition is and to establish a distinction between the basic and specialised meaning of a definition. | Task 1: Video and questionnaire | *Presentation task*: first contact with definitions. | 20' | Listening |
| | | Task 2: basic meaning vs specialised meaning | *Practice task*: working with the connection between both meanings. | 20' | Writing |
| | | Task 3: checklist | *Assessment task*: perception checklist. | 5' | Reading |
| Phase 2 | To work with sentence definitions: identifying their main elements, differentiating terms from the same class, and providing precise and accurate definitions. Students will be asked to produce their own sentence definitions. | Task 4: identifying the main parts of sentence definitions | *Practice task*: identifying the main elements of sentence definitions. | 20'-30' | Reading |
| | | Task 5: different terms for the same class | *Practice task:* identifying different concepts within the same class. | 20'-30' | Reading and writing |
| | | Task 6: providing precise definitions | Production task: writing sentence definitions to provide a precise class. | 30'-40' | Writing |
| | | Task 7: checklist | *Assessment task*: perception checklist. | 5' | Reading |

(*Continued*)

**Table 10.** Continued

| Phase | Aim | Tasks | Description | Time | Typology |
|---|---|---|---|---|---|
| Phase 3 | To work with extended definitions: identifying their main elements and differentiating them from sentence definitions. | Task 8: identifying the main parts of extended definitions | *Practice task*: identifying the general definition and the specific parts of extended definitions. | 20’ | Reading |
| | | Task 9: extending your definitions | *Production task:* changing task 6 sentence definitions to extended ones. | 30’ | Writing |
| | | Task 10: checklist | *Assessment task*: perception checklist. | 5’ | Reading |
| Phase 4 | To focus on the language that should be used in definitions. Students will become familiar with defining verbs and learn how to avoid redundancy in definitions. | Task 11: avoiding redundancy | *Practice task*: changing given definitions into more precise ones. | 20’ | Writing |
| | | Task 12: choosing the most suitable verb | *Practice task:* filling definitions with the correct defining verb. | 20’ | Reading and writing |
| | | Task 13: checklist | *Assessment task*: perception checklist | 5’ | Reading |
| Phase 5 | To bring together all the knowledge acquired in the module. Students will learn how to identify definitions and to create their own glossary. | Task 14: distinguishing between definition types | *Practice task:* looking for definitions in a longer text and categorising them. | 45’ | Reading |
| | | Task 15: creating a glossary | *Production task:* starting a glossary with the terms learnt in the module. | 45’ | Writing |
| | | Task 16: checklist | *Assessment task*: perception checklist | 5’ | Reading |

### *Phase 1: Warm-up: understanding and writing definitions*

The main learning aim of this phase is for students to become familiar with the basic aspects needed before creating definitions. This first step consists in learning what a definition is, what is needed to write a definition (elements) and different types of definitions.

Phase 1 will bc completed in 45 minutes through three different tasks:

- Task 1 is a presentation task for students to become familiar with definitions (listening activity).
- Task 2 is a practice task for students to understand the difference between basic meanings and specialised meanings (reading and writing activity).
- Task 3 is a checklist to assess understanding (reading activity).

In the presentation task (task 1), students will be asked to watch the introductory video about definitions (https://www.youtube.com/watch?v=I2S1spAdMk4&ab_channel=LanguageEducationandResearchNetwork) and answer a questionnaire comprising seven multiple-choice questions. This is the first time the concept of 'definition' is introduced.

In task (task 2), students will explore the possible figurative connections between the basic and the specialised meanings of terms in their field of study. Then they will be asked to write the specific definition and contrast it with its basic meaning in everyday English (using a dictionary).

Finally, in the assessment task (task 3), students can assess their own learning, checking if they have properly understood the main ideas presented in this phase.

### Task 1. Questionnaire on the theoretical video

1. **What is a definition?**
   a. A statement of the meaning of a word, an expression, a sign or a symbol.
   b. A short piece of work to add to your summaries and outlines.
   c. The starting point for other productions.
   d. None of the above.

2. **Which one of these is NOT an element of a definition?**
   a. Class.
   b. Term.
   c. Spelling.
   d. Characteristics.
3. **What is the 'class' of a definition?**
   a. The concept being defined.
   b. Extra knowledge that you have about the term.
   c. The category of the term.
   d. Specific characteristics of the term.
4. **What is the 'specialised meaning' of a word?**
   a. How it is usually known.
   b. How it is known in a specific field.
   c. How it is known in Linguistics.
   d. How it appears in the dictionary.
5. **Which one of these options contains the different types of definitions?**
   a. Specialised, glosses and extended definitions.
   b. General, short and specialised definitions.
   c. Glosses, sentence and specialised definitions.
   d. Glosses, sentence and extended definitions.
6. **Which one of these is NOT a sentence definition?**
   a. A synonym is a word or phrase that has the same or nearly the same meaning as another word or phrase in the same language.
   b. An illusion is an idea or belief that is not true.
   c. An app is a computer program that is designed for a particular purpose.
   d. A big rock (called a boulder).
7. **Which one of these verbs is NOT a defining verb?**
   a. Refer.
   b. Argue.
   c. Call.
   d. Name.

### Task 2. Basic meaning vs specialised meaning

*Take a look at the word tongue. We can find the following meanings in the Macmillan dictionary (online edition: https://www.macmillandictionary.com/):*

1. *Basic meaning: the long soft piece of flesh fixed to the bottom of your mouth that you use for tasting, speaking etc. E.g. I burnt my tongue on the hot coffee.*
2. *Specialised meaning: a language. E.g. your native tongue: English was clearly not his native tongue.*

*There seems to be a figurative (metonymic) connection between these two meanings: one of the functions of our tongue is helping us to talk, that is, to produce the language we speak.*

- *Can you think of a term in your field of study with a meaning that is different from the most frequent one in everyday English?*
- *Write that specific definition and, using the MacMillan Dictionary (https://www.macmillandictionary.com/) or any other dictionary of your preference, contrast it with its basic meaning in everyday English.*
- *Can you see any connection between both meanings?*

### Task 3. Checklist phase 1 checklist.

1. **I have learnt what a definition is**
   a. Yes
   b. No
2. **I know the main types of definitions.**
   a. Yes
   b. No
3. **I can distinguish between basic and specialised meaning.**
   a. Yes
   b. No
4. **I can identify the elements of definitions.**
   a. Yes
   b. No

### *Phase 2: Sentence definitions*

The main aim of phase 2 is to provide some insights into the most common strategies for writing sentence definitions. Students will identify the main elements and characteristics of sentence definitions: term, class and specific details, as well as how to structure these in order to start writing their definitions.

Phase 2 will be completed in 1 and a half hours through four different tasks:

- Task 4 is a practice task to identify the main elements of sentence definitions (reading activity).
- Task 5 is a practice task to identify different terms from the same class (reading and writing activity).
- Task 6 is a production task for students to write their own definitions (writing activity).
- Task 7 is a checklist to assess understanding (reading activity).

In the first practice task (task 4), students will have to identify the term, the class, and the specific characteristics of sentence definitions. After completing the task, they will be provided with a model answer (see 'answer key').

In task 5, students will work with the words provided in task 4. They will have to think about other concepts that belong to the same class.

In the production task (task 6), students will write their own definitions for the first time in the module. They will have to think about accurate ways of describing the terms provided in the task (see 'Words to define') and when they have finished, they can check the model answer (see 'answer key').

Finally, in task 7, students can assess their own learning, checking if they have properly understood the contents of the phase.

### Task 4. Identifying the main parts of sentence definitions

*Sentence definitions contain a term, a class and some specific information. Take this sentence as an example: 'a plane is a vehicle designed for air travel, with wings and one or more engines'.*

*The term that is being defined would be 'plane', which belongs to a class, 'vehicle'. After the class has been presented, the definition is completed with a simple characteristic (for instance, 'with wings and one or more engines').*

*In this task, you will have to identify the term, the class and the specific detail in these sentence definitions below.*

- *How are these elements joined together in the definition?*
- *In your opinion, which definition is the most precise? Why?*

Materials for Task 4. 'Identifying the main parts of sentence definitions'

- **Some definitions**

  – *A watermelon is a large round fruit that has a hard green skin outside and is red with small black seeds inside.*
  – *A dictionary is a reference resource which provides information about words and their meanings, uses, and pronunciations.*
  – *Metal is a hard element that exists naturally in the ground or in rock, for example lead, gold, or iron.*
  – *A basement is the part of a building that is partly or completely below the level of the ground.*
  – *A skirt is a piece of clothing that covers the lower part of the body and part or all of the legs.*
  – *A robot is a machine that can do work by itself, often work that humans do.*

(Source: https://www.macmillandictionary.com/)

## Task 5. Different terms for the same class

*A class includes several terms. If we take the same example of the definition of 'plane', we can think about other 'vehicles', for instance 'cars'. The definition of 'car' would be 'a road vehicle with an engine, four wheels, and seats for a small number of people'. We can see that it is different from a plane because of the specific detail in the sentence definition, which provides a different characteristic.*

*Think about the words provided in exercise 4:*

- *Can you think about other terms that belong to the same class?*
- *How are they different from the terms in exercise 4?*

### Task 6. Providing precise definitions

*When giving a definition, we should be as precise as possible. Take a look at these definitions of 'car':*

> *Definition 1: a road vehicle with an engine, four wheels, and seats for a small number of people.*
> *Definition 2: a vehicle with seats for a small number of people.*

*Which one of these definitions is more precise? Obviously, definition 1 provides more information about the term. The class in the first definition is longer ('road vehicle' instead of just 'vehicle') and there are more details.*

*Think about a precise class for the following words. Then, try to define all of them, adding a specific detail:*

- *A glossary:*
- *A subject:*
- *Psychology:*
- *An outline:*
- *Self-assessment:*
- *English:*
- *One of your own:*

### Task 7. Checklist phase 2

1. **I understand what a sentence definition is.**
   a) Yes
   b) No
2. **I can identify the elements in sentence definitions.**
   a) Yes
   b) No
3. **I am able to produce precise sentence definitions.**
   a) Yes
   b) No

### *Phase 3: Extended definitions*

The main learning aim of this phase is to provide students with some insights into the most common strategies for writing extended definitions. Students will identify the main elements and characteristics of extended definitions: general definition and specific details as well as how to extend sentence definitions.

Phase 3 will be completed in 1 hour through three different tasks:

- Task 8 is a practice task for students to identify the main parts of extended definitions (reading activity).
- Task 9 is a production task in which students will extend their own definitions (writing activity).
- Task 10 is a checklist to assess understanding (reading activity).

In the practice task (task 8), students will have to identify the main elements of several extended definitions and make them more accurate. Students will need the material provided in 'Words to define', and after finishing the task, they can check the model answer (see 'answer key').

In task 9, students will be asked to extend the sentence definitions they wrote in task 6.

Finally, in task 10, students can assess their own learning, checking if they have understood the contents of the phase.

### Task 8. Identifying the main parts of extended definitions

*This is an example of an extended definition:*

*'**Glasses** are vision eyewear, consisting of glass or hard plastic lenses mounted in a frame that holds them in front of a person's eyes. Glasses are typically used for vision correction, such as with reading glasses and glasses used for nearsightedness, however, without the specialized lenses, they are sometimes used for cosmetic purposes.'*

*You could have ended your definition in the first sentence, making it a sentence definition. However, you can be more specific and add the details that you know.*

*Take a look at these extended definitions below:*

- *Can you make a distinction between what would be the general definition (sentence definition) and the specific part of it?*

- *Is the specific part of the definition necessary? Do you think it provides relevant information?*
- *Would you add something else to the definitions to make them more accurate?*

**Material for Task 8. 'Identifying the main parts of extended definitions'**

- ***Pollution*** *is a form of environmental contamination resulting from human activity. Some common forms of pollution are wastes from the burning of fossil fuels and sewage running into rivers. Even litter and excessive noise can be considered forms of pollution.*
- *A* ***light bulb*** *is an electric light with a wire filament heated until it glows. The filament is enclosed in a glass bulb with a vacuum or inert gas to protect the filament from oxidation. Current is supplied to the filament by terminals or wires embedded in the glass. A bulb socket provides mechanical support and electrical connections.*
- ***Painting*** *is the practice of applying paint, pigment, colour or other medium to a solid surface. The medium is commonly applied to the base with a brush, but other implements, such as knives, sponges, and airbrushes, can be used. In art, the term painting describes both the act and the result of the action (the final work is called 'a painting').*
- *A* ***videotape*** *is magnetic tape used for storing video and usually sound in addition. Information stored can be in the form of either an analogue signal or digital signal. Videotape is used in both video tape recorders (VTRs) or, more commonly, videocassette recorders (VCRs) and camcorders.*
- *A* ***flower*** *is the reproductive structure found in flowering plants (plants of the division Magnoliophyta, also called angiosperms). The biological function of a flower is to facilitate reproduction, usually by providing a mechanism for the union of sperm with eggs.*

## Task 9. Extending your definitions

*This is a sentence definition: '***Painting*** *is the practice of applying paint, pigment, colour or other medium to a solid surface'.*

*A way of transforming it into an extended definition would be by adding more features, like this: 'The medium is commonly applied to the base with a brush, but other implements, such as knives, sponges, and airbrushes, can be used'.*

*This is what you are asked to do in this task. Look at the sentence definitions you wrote in task 6. Can you think of any more characteristics for these terms? Try to expand all the definitions, making them extended ones.*

**Task 10. Checklist phase 3 checklist**

1. **I know the difference between a sentence and an extended definition.**
   a. Yes
   b. No
2. **I can identify the elements of an extended definition.**
   a. Yes
   b. No
3. **I am able to extend my definitions.**
   a. Yes
   b. No

***Phase 4: The language of definitions***

The main learning goal of this phase is to be able to use the most precise language possible when writing definitions. Students will learn how to avoid redundancy and how to make use of the defining verbs.

Phase 4 will be completed in 1 hour and a half through three different tasks:

- Task 11 is a practice task to learn how to avoid redundancy (reading and writing activity).
- Task 12 is a practice task for students to learn to use the most suitable verb in different definitions (reading and writing activity).
- Task 13 is a checklist to assess understanding (reading activity).

In the first practice task (task 11), students will have to rephrase several redundant definitions (by avoiding using the term in the definition). Students will need the materials provided in 'Definitions 1', and after finishing the task, they can check the model answer (see 'answer key').

In task 12, students will be provided with various definitions with gaps. They will have to fill in the gaps using an appropriate defining verb. After completing the task with the materials provided in 'Definitions 2', they will be given a model answer (see 'answer key').

Finally, in task 13, students can assess their own learning, checking if they have properly understood the contents of the phase.

## Task 11. Avoiding redundancy

*Definitions should be as precise as possible. Therefore, it is important to avoid using any form of the term to be defined in a definition to avoid redundancy.*

*Take a look at this definition: 'a* ***drink*** *is an amount of liquid that, when drunk, is taken into the body'. As you can see, it does not provide much information, and the term is not fully defined. To make this definition more appropriate, we can say 'is taken into the body through the mouth' instead of 'when drunk'.*

*Change these redundant definitions by avoiding the use of the term. After you have changed the definitions, you can check the model answer.*

| Materials for Task 11. 'Avoiding redundancy' |
|---|

- **Paving***: paving is a paved area, or material used to pave an area.*
- **Sight***: sight is the ability to see.*
- **Song***: a song is a short piece of music with words that are sung.*
- **Painting***: a painting is a picture made using paint.*
- **Erosion***: erosion is the process during which the surface of the Earth erodes*

## Task 12. Choosing the most suitable verb

*As you will be aware by now, we can use different verbs to define words. Which verb fits better in these definitions? Choose among the defining verbs: 'define', 'refer', 'known', 'name', 'denote', 'call'. You will need to modify the verbal tenses to make them fit.*

## Materials for Task 12. 'Choosing the most suitable verb'

- Procrastination ............... to deliberately putting off one's intended actions.
- The term 'road rage' is ............... in the Oxford English Dictionary as 'violent anger caused by the stress and frustration of driving in heavy traffic'.
- A study of the geologic record of past seismic activities is ........... paleoseismology.
- The natural increase in temperature as the depth increases is ............... as the geothermal gradient.
- A partitive phrase is a construction that ............... part of a whole.
- The activity of visiting interesting places, especially by people on holiday is ............... sightseeing.
- Chakras .......... to energy points that connect the various bodies each of us inhabit.
- Total government dependency is .......... as the share of Americans receiving one or more federal benefit payments.
- The share of Americans receiving one or more federal benefit payments is .......... as total government dependency.

## Task 13. Checklist phase 4

1. **I can avoid redundancy when defining words**
   a. Yes
   b. No
2. **I can use defining verbs when creating my definitions**
   a. Yes
   b. No
3. **I can distinguish between the purposes of the defining verbs**
   a. Yes
   b. No

### *Phase 5: Gathering information and defining*

The main learning aim of this phase is for students to be able to bring together all the knowledge acquired in the module. Students will learn how to identify definitions and to create their own glossary.

Phase 5 will be completed in 1 hour and a half through three different tasks:

- Task 14 is a practice task in which students look for definitions in a text and categorise them.
- Task 15 is a production task in which students start a glossary with the terms learnt in the module.
- Task 16 is perception checklist to assess understanding.

In the first practice task (task 14), students will be asked to skim through one or two journal articles recommended in their subjects, looking for definitions. They must categorize them as one of the types described using the 'classification grid' provided in the materials.

In task 15, students will start their own glossary with the terms covered in the module.

Finally, in task 16, students can assess their own learning, checking if they have properly understood the contents of the phase.

### Task 14. Distinguishing between definition types

*Skim through one or two journal articles recommended to you by your university lecturers in different subjects of your degree programme and look for definitions. Highlight any definitions you find and try to categorize them as one of the types described. You can use the classification grid below (or modify it if you prefer).*

- *In which section of the article did you find the definitions?*
- *Why do you think they appear there?*

Materials for Task 14. 'Distinguishing between definition types'

- **Classification grid**

| **Term** | **Definition** | **Type of definition (tick)** | | |
|---|---|---|---|---|
| | | **Short** | **Sentence** | **Extended** |
| | | | | |
| | | | | |

| Term | Definition | Type of definition (tick) | | |
|---|---|---|---|---|
| | | Short | Sentence | Extended |
| | | | | |
| | | | | |

**Task 15. Creating a glossary**

*Start a glossary with all the definitions of key terms that appear in the tasks in this module. You can add the definitions that are already in the module and provide your own with terms that you consider important.*

*Your glossary will have to contain approximately 20 words. Try to include at least 5 definitions of your own. You can add any type of definition.*

**Task 16. Phase 5 checklist**

1. **I am able to recognize definitions in a longer text.**
   a. Yes
   b. No
2. **I can define any type of word.**
   a. Yes
   b. No
3. **I can create my own glossary.**
   a. Yes
   b. No

Table 11 shows a rubric that has been developed to assess this module and that can be used as a self-assessment, peer-assessment tool for students as well as an evaluation tool for instructors if the module is taught in a class.

*External sources for materials in this module*

– https://www.macmillandictionary.com/dictionary/british/
– https://dictionary.cambridge.org/

### 2.2.3.4. Rubric for assessment

**Table 11.** Rubric to assess module 2 'Writing definitions'

| Element | Excellent (4) | Good (3) | Fair (2) | Poor (1) |
|---|---|---|---|---|
| **Content Elements** | | | | |
| Types of definitions | The student is able to distinguish between glosses, sentence definition, and extended definitions. | The student can distinguish at least two types of definitions. | The student is able to provide at least one type of definition. | The different types of definitions are not distinguished. |
| Definition formats | The definition includes all the basic elements: term, class, and features. Basic and specialised meaning are present. | The definition is mostly appropriate and can be easily understood, but one of the basic elements is missing. | The definition is easily understood, but the student does not differentiate between basic and specialised meaning. | The definition does not include the basic elements, and there is not a clear distinction between basic and specialised meaning. |
| **Language Elements** | | | | |
| Defining verbs | The student is able to include different defining verbs according to the type of definition and its function. | The student is able to identify the purpose of some defining verbs, although sometimes they use the same one for different purposes. | Defining verbs are included, but these do not fit the definitions. | Defining verbs are not included. |
| Synthesis of the definition | The definition is precise and redundancy is avoided. | The definition could be more precise, but redundancy is avoided, and the main characteristics of the term are clear. | Even though the definition is easily understood, it is redundant (inclusion of the term in the actual definition). | The definition is redundant and inaccurate. |

### *2.2.4. Module 3: Writing summaries*

#### 2.2.4.1. Overview and aims

This module aims to provide students with the fundamental knowledge and tools to create summaries. University students are expected to understand summaries of academic texts and they are also often asked to summarise academic texts (journal articles, book chapters, and, less frequently, books) themselves. They may also need to summarise from oral input (e.g., a lecture or a presentation). Swales and Feak (2012, p. 188) state that "in an academic setting especially, summaries can form an essential part of our preparation for an exam, a class discussion, a research paper, a thesis, or a dissertation".

When reading a summary, a university student should be able to decide whether the publication is worth reading. When writing a summary of their own work (e.g. at the end of the introductory section of a BA dissertation), they should be able to provide readers with a concise preview of what it is to come without discussing the specific details.

An academic summary is different from an abstract in that they have different objectives and requirements. We will deal with abstracts in module 6.

This topic will be introduced through four different self-study phases, implementing both theoretical aspects and practical exercises under the principles of self-study and self-assessment. In short, the goal of this module is to provide the knowledge necessary to understand and write summaries.

The interactive version of the module developed in *Genial.ly* can be accessed here: https://view.genial.ly/5fd9d1a43c971e0d6598c81b/learning-experience-didactic-unit-writing-summariesmodule

And the introductory video hosted in our *L2EARN* channel in YouTube is also freely available: https://www.youtube.com/watch?v=UXjehxyA4CU&t=311s

At the end of this module, students will be able to:

- Create their own summary of a given text without any type of guidance or support.
- Identify and link the main ideas of a text.

- Use the correct language structures to write an adequate summary.
- Self-assess their own performance at the end of each phase.

In addition, students will be able to understand written input as well as produce written output related to the content objectives.

The module is designed to be completed in three and a half hours, so the student workload should not be longer than this. According to the Common European Framework of Reference (CEFR), it is adapted to the B2 level (English) and will contribute to the development of the following skills: spoken comprehension, written comprehension and written production.

### 2.2.4.2. Learning outcomes

The *language skills (CEFR)* that are going to be dealt with in this module are the following:

1. Comprehension:
   a) Written:
      - Can scan quickly through long and complex texts, locating relevant details.
      - Can understand articles and reports concerned with contemporary problems in which the writers adopt particular stances, or viewpoints.
      - Can recognise when a text provides factual information, and when it seeks to convince readers of something.
      - Can recognise different structures in discursive text: contrasting arguments, problem-solution presentation, and cause-effect relationships.

   b) Spoken:
      - Can understand recordings in the standard form of the language likely to be encountered in social, professional, or academic life and identify speaker viewpoints and attitudes as well as the information content.
2. Production:
   a) Written:
      - Can write clear, detailed texts on a variety of subjects related to his/her field of interest, synthesising, and

evaluating information and arguments from a number of sources.
- Can write an essay or report that develops an argument systematically with appropriate highlighting of significant points and relevant supporting detail.
- Can synthesise information and arguments from a number of sources.
- Can often retrospectively self-correct his/her occasional 'slips' or non-systematic errors and minor flaws in sentence structure.

In addition, there are some other *functions* that will be covered:

- Summarising information.
- Referring to authors.
- Paraphrasing.

Finally, the *language foci* will be:

- Connectors.
- Reporting verbs.
- Synonyms.
- Antonyms.

#### 2.2.4.3. Contents: Phases and tasks

Table 12 below shows the activities to be carried out in the module.

**Table 12.** List of activities for module 3 'Writing summaries'

| Phase | Aim | Tasks | Description | Time | Typology |
|---|---|---|---|---|---|
| Phase 1 | To introduce what a summary is and its main characteristics. | Task 1: Video and questionnaire | *Presentation task*: first contact with summaries. | 20' | Listening |
| | | Task 2: checklist | *Assessment task*: perception checklist | 5' | Reading |
| Phase 2 | To present the previous steps that should be carried out before writing a summary. Students will be asked to work with summaries, identifying their characteristics and structure and creating outlines with the main information. | Task 3: elements of a summary. | *Practice task*: reading a summary and identifying its main elements. | 20' | Reading. |
| | | Task 4: creating an outline. | *Practice task*: creating an outline from a summary. | 40' | Reading and writing |
| | | Task 5: checklist | *Assessment task*: perception checklist. | 5' | Reading |
| Phase 3 | To focus on the use of language structures that are suitable and appropriate for summaries. Students will work with connectors and reporting verbs, learning how to paraphrase, link and introduce the main ideas of a summary and quote authors. | Task 6: reporting verbs when referring to authors. | *Practice task:* analysing the purpose of different sentences, according to the reporting verb used. | 30' | Reading |
| | | Task 7: the language of summaries. | *Practice task*: analysing the language of a summary, changing some language structures. | 30' | Reading and writing |
| | | Task 8: checklist | *Assessment task*: perception checklist. | 5' | Reading |
| Phase 4 | To assess students' construction of their own summary. Learners will also self-assess their own production. | Task 9: writing a summary in under 120 words | *Production task*: writing a summary of a previously worked text. | 50' | Writing |
| | | Task 10: checking the summary | *Assessment task:* checking your summary. | 10' | Reading |
| | | Task 11: checklist | *Assessment task*: perception checklist. | 5' | Reading |

### *Phase 1: Warm-up phase*

The main learning goal of this phase is for students to become familiar with the basic aspects needed before writing a summary. This first step consists in learning what a summary is, the language structures that should be included in it, as well as the essential steps required in the summary process.

Phase 1 will be completed in 30 minutes through two different tasks:

- Task 1 is a presentation task for students to understand and write summaries (reading and listening activity).
- Task 2 is a checklist to assess understanding (reading activity).

In the presentation task (task 1), students will be asked to watch the introductory video about summaries (https://www.youtube.com/watch?v=UXjehxyA4CU&t=311s) and answer a questionnaire comprising five multiple-choice questions. This is the first time the concept of summaries is introduced.

In task 2, students can assess their own learning by checking if they have properly understood the main ideas presented in the video.

**Task 1. Questionnaire on the theoretical video: Understanding and writing summaries.**

1. **What is a summary?**
   a. A summary is a shortened or condensed version of a reading.
   b. A short piece of writing by a student on a particular subject.
   c. A piece of writing about a particular subject that is published in a newspaper or magazine.
   d. A spoken or written account that gives information about a particular subject, situation, or event.
2. **What does a summary include?**
   a. It should include examples and secondary ideas.
   b. It should contain all the ideas reflected in the original text.
   c. It should only include the most important concepts or ideas.
   d. It should include direct quotes.

3. **What is the purpose of this expression?** *The second/third claim is based on…*
   a. Starting your summary.
   b. Moving to the next section.
   c. Referring to the author's ideas.
   d. Concluding.
4. **Which type of language should you use when writing your summary?**
   a. Repetition of the author's sentences.
   b. Arguments to give your opinion.
   c. Synonyms, antonyms and reporting verbs.
   d. Arguments for both sides in the discussion.
5. **Some things should be avoided when writing a summary, namely…**
   a. Using formal language.
   b. Repetition of similar ideas and inclusion of minor details and direct quotes.
   c. Paraphrasing.
   d. Identification of the author in the first sentence.

**Task 2. Checklist warm-up phase**

1. **I have learnt what a summary is.**
   a. Yes
   b. No
2. **I have learned about the elements and main characteristics of a summary.**
   a. Yes
   b. No
3. **I have learned about the language used in summaries.**
   a. Yes
   b. No
4. **I am able to identify and understand the different phases in the summary process.**
   a. Yes
   b. No

### *Phase 2: Identifying the elements of a summary*

The aim of this phase is to provide some insights into the most common strategies for identifying the main parts of a summary (main ideas, supporting points, details and irrelevant information) as well as how to structure these in order to start writing a summary.

Phase 2 will be completed in 1 hour through three different tasks:

- Task 3 is a practice task for students to identify the main ideas of a text (reading and writing activity).
- Task 4 is also a practice task for students to (reading and writing activity).
- Task 5 is a checklist to assess understanding (reading activity).

In the first practice task (task 3), students are asked to read a summary and underline its main elements. Students will need the material provided in 'Sample summary 1', and after finishing the task, they can check the model answer (see 'answer key').

In task 4, students will be referred back to the outlines provided in the introductory module. The is to the create their own outline of the summary provided in task 3 and compare it with those two outlines. When completing the task, they will be provided with a model answer (see 'answer key').

Finally, in task 5, students can assess their own learning, checking if they have properly understood the contents of the phase.

### Task 3. Elements of a summary

*Identify the main parts of this summary of the extract by Llinares et al. (2012) that was presented in the introductory module 'Creating outlines'. Remember that the main parts of a summary are the following: introduction, main ideas, supporting ideas, details and conclusion. In your opinion, is there any irrelevant information? Is there anything missing?*

## Materials for Task 3. 'Elements of a summary'

- **Summary**

In this extract from *The Role of Language in CLIL* by Llinares, Morton and Whittaker (2012), the authors highlight the important role of writing when learning in Content and Language Integrated Learning (CLIL) contexts. Llinares and her colleagues state that although a great emphasis is put on spoken language in CLIL lessons, working on writing is essential as it provides learners not only with information but also with models of the language they need to learn. The authors argue that writing in a foreign language is a complex, difficult process that requires effort on the part of the learners and making decisions at the levels of genre and register. They report that research shows that writing allows reflection -leaving a permanent trace in the writer-, knowledge creation -expanding language resources-, and discovery -finding the suitable language in the L2. Finally, the authors emphasise the importance of helping CLIL learners in the transition from the spoken to the written mode through both planned and spontaneous register scaffolding.

Source: Own elaboration

## Task 4. Analysing the elements of a summary: Creating an outline

*In the introductory module ('Creating outlines'), you were provided with some examples of outlines for the original extract by Llinares et al. (2012). Can you now create your own outline from the summary you have been working with in Task 3? In what ways is it similar to and different from the outlines in the introductory module?*

## Task 5. Checklist phase 2

## Questions:

1. **I can identify the main ideas in a text.**
   a. Yes
   b. No
2. **I can identify supporting ideas and details in a text.**
   a. Yes
   b. No
3. **I can create an outline to write my summary.**
   a. Yes
   b. No

### *Phase 3: The language of summaries*

The main learning objective of this phase is to focus on the language structures needed to write a summary. It aims to analyse connectors, reporting verbs and other paraphrasing structures.

Phase 3 will be completed in 1 hour through three different activities:

- Task 6 is a practice task for students to learn how to use reporting verbs when referring to authors (reading activity).
- Task 7 is also a practice task focused on the language of summaries (reading activity).
- Task 8 is a checklist to assess understanding (reading activity).

In the first practice task (task 6), students will analyse different sentences that refer to authors' ideas. They will classify them according to their purpose, focusing on the reporting verb that is being used. Students will need the material provided in 'Reporting verbs when referring to authors', and after finishing the task, they can check the model answer (see 'answer key').

In task 7, students are asked to identify the language structures in a summary, analysing their purposes. After that, they will replace them with others that make sense.

When completing the task with the materials provided in 'Summary', they can check a model answer (see 'answer key').

Finally, in task 8, students can assess their own learning, checking if they have properly understood the contents of the phase.

### Task 6. Reporting verbs when referring to authors

*Focus on the reporting verbs in these sentences. What purpose do these sentences have? Can you classify them according to the grid?*

## Materials for Task 6. 'Reporting verbs when referring to authors'

- **Sentences**
  - Chomsky **casted doubt on / questioned** earlier views about language
  - In her latest book, Littlemore **mentions** some new research in the field
  - Lakoff & Johnson **emphasised** / **highlighted** / **stressed** the importance of metaphor in language and thought.
  - Hume **suggested/implied** that passions and not reason guide human behaviour
  - Newton's first law **states** that/ **According to** Newton's first law, an object will not change its motion unless a force acts on it.
  - Galilei **claimed / asserted / contended / maintained / declared** that the Earth orbits the Sun.
  - Martin Luther King **argued** that all races should always be treated equally to white people.
  - Einstein **showed/demonstrated** the motion of small particles suspended in a stationary liquid, providing empirical evidence for the atomic theory.
- **Grid**

| Purpose | Sentence (S) |
|---|---|
| **To say indirectly** | (1 sentences) |
| **To say directly** | (1 sentence) |
| **To say something is true** | (2 sentences) |
| **To give arguments or reasons** | (1 sentence) |
| **To suggest something is inaccurate** | (1 sentences) |
| **To give importance** | (1 sentences) |
| **To refer to briefly** | (1 sentences) |

## Task 7. The language of summaries

*Let's work with the summary in task 3 again. However, this time you will have to focus on the language structures used by the author:*

- *Underline them*
- *Identify their purpose.*

| Materials for Task 7. The language of summaries |
|---|

See the text in the materials for Task 3 above.

## Task 8. Checklist phase 3

1. **I can identify the purpose of different reporting verbs.**
   a. Yes
   b. No
2. **I can quote authors in my summary.**
   a. Yes
   b. No
3. **I can identify the main language structures used to connect ideas in a summary.**
   a. Yes
   b. No
4. **I am able to use the language of summaries.**
   a. Yes
   b. No

### *Phase 4: Writing your own summary*

The main learning aim of this phase is for students to be able to create a summary of less than 120 words of a previously studied text given (with the tools provided). Moreover, students will be able to self-assess their work with the checklist provided.

Phase 4 will be completed in 1 hour through three different tasks:

- Task 9 is a production task in which students will write their own summary (writing activity).
- Task 10 is an assessment task for students to check the summary they have written (reading activity).
- Task 11 is a checklist to assess understanding (reading activity).

In the production task (task 9), students will be asked to read a text related to their field of specialisation (preferably one that has been previously studied in class). They have to create their own summary of the text, in under 120 words.

In task 10, students will check the summary they prepared for the previous task. They will be asked to evaluate whether they have included the main ideas, and whether the summary supports the author's key points, together with the language used, by completing a grid (see 'Self-assessment grid' below).

Finally, in task 11, students can assess their own learning, checking if they have properly understood the contents of the phase.

### TASK 9. Write your summary in less than 120 words

*In this task, you will have to summarise a text that you have already studied in class. Since you are already familiar with it, and its topic belongs to your field of study, the task will be easy. However, there are some guidelines that can help you write your summary. Remember to…*

1. *Read the text carefully – know the text in (great) detail!*
2. *Identify important ideas*
3. *Try to distinguish main ideas from supporting ideas*
4. *Make notes and create an outline*
5. *Write your summary in less than 120 words (in your own words!)*
6. *Check the text.*

### Task 10. Checking your summary

*Check your summary (the one you prepared for task 9) and complete the following 'self-assessment grid'*

| **Statement** | **Yes** | **No** |
|---|---|---|
| **My summary includes a clear presentation of the main ideas.** | | |
| **I have added support for these ideas (supporting ideas and details).** | | |
| **I have included an introductory paragraph, stating the name of the author and publication.** | | |
| **I have avoided plagiarism in my summary.** | | |

| Statement | Yes | No |
|---|---|---|
| **I have paraphrased the author's ideas (using synonyms, antonyms and reporting verbs).** | | |
| **I have used connectors to link my ideas.** | | |
| **I have quoted the author when necessary.** | | |
| **I have included a conclusion at the end of my summary.** | | |

*With these answers in mind, how can you improve your summary? Would you include something else?*

## Task 11. Checklist phase 4

1. **I can write my own summary following the steps involved in the summary process.**
   a. Yes
   b. No
2. **I can include the essential language structures for a good summary.**
   a. Yes
   b. No
3. **I can paraphrase and quote authors when needed.**
   a. Yes
   b. No
4. **I have completed all the tasks in the "Writing summaries" module.**
   a. Yes
   b. No

Table 13 shows a rubric that has been developed to assess this module and that can be used as a self-assessment, peer-assessment tool for students as well as an evaluation tool for instructors if the module is taught in a class.

### 2.2.4.4. Rubric for assessment

**Table 13.** Rubric to assess module 3 'Writing summaries'

| Element | Excellent (4) | Good (3) | Fair (2) | Poor (1) |
|---|---|---|---|---|
| **Content Elements** | | | | |
| Completeness | All the ideas of the original text are included. | Most of the ideas of the original text are included. | Some ideas of the original text are included. | Only one idea of the original text is included. |
| Synthesis of information | The information is appropriately synthesised, it clearly reflects the main and supporting ideas in the text, and is written in the student's own words. | The information is partly synthesised and is written in the student's own words. | The information is poorly synthesised and is only partly written in the student's own words. | The information is not synthesised, and is not written in the student's own words. |
| Organization of the summary and readability | It includes the required five main elements: an introduction, main and supporting ideas, details, and a conclusion. It is written in paragraph form. | It includes an introduction, main and supporting ideas and a conclusion. It is written in paragraph form. | It only includes three of the main elements. It is only partly written in paragraph form. | It does not include an introduction or a conclusion. It focuses on only one idea and/or it is not written in paragraph form. |
| **Language Elements** | | | | |
| Use of reporting verbs and/or adverbs | A wide variety of reporting verbs and/or adverbs are included and each of them has the correct function. | Only a couple of reporting verbs and/or adverbs with the correct function are included. Some of them are repeated. | Although some reporting verbs and/or adverbs are included, they do not render the author's main ideas. | No reporting verbs and/or adverbs to render the author's main ideas are included. |
| Paraphrasing the initial text and referring to authors | The authors' ideas are paraphrased, and they are correctly referenced. | A few sentences are directly copied from the author, but these are correctly referenced. | Some ideas from the text are paraphrased but are not referenced. | Parts of the summary are sentences copied from the author without references. |
| Inclusion of linking words | A wide variety of linking words are included: to start a summary, move to the next section, connect ideas, refer to the author's main ideas, and to conclude | Sufficient linking words are included. | Some linking words are included. | Linking words barely appear or are not included at all. |

### *2.2.5. Module 4: Reporting data*

#### **2.2.5.1. Overview and aims**

This module aims to provide students with the fundamental knowledge and tools to report data.

Reporting data is an important learning skill that students will find very useful at university. Swales and Feak (2012) devote a section of their book to data commentary stating that reporting data is an essential part of many academic writing tasks, particularly, in some specific fields such as Engineering. In my view, interpreting data from different sources to have informed opinions about different issues is an essential skill for anybody nowadays. In the final stages of university undergraduate programmes and in most post-graduate degrees, students are often asked to become initiated in research by formulating hypotheses or more specific research questions based on previous findings from the literature in their specific fields. They need to develop a methodology which often includes collecting, interpreting, and reporting their own data. And this applies to the different research areas: Sciences, Health Science, Social Sciences and Humanities.

In this module, students will be first confronted with how graphs display information visually by presenting the most common types of graphs: line graphs, bar graphs, histograms, circle graphs, and stacked bar graphs. It is important to recognize the main differences between them to be able to make correct interpretations and, at a later stage, to choose the most appropriate for their own purposes when analysing the trends in their own data and reporting.

The interactive version of the module developed in *Genial.ly* can be accessed here: https://view.genial.ly/605867e01e77ea0d0e1d3e92/learning-experience-didactic-unit-reporting-datamodule

And the introductory video (divided into two parts) hosted in our *L2EARN* channel in YouTube is also available:

Part I. https://www.youtube.com/watch?v=iUKl44062OA

Part II. https://www.youtube.com/watch?v=9CslIdoicYI&t=1s

At the end of this module, students will be able to:

- Describe trends and refer to visuals orally and in written form.
- Compare graphs and trends in English.

- Correctly use basic vocabulary to describe trends, distinguishing between verbs, nouns and adverbs.
- Interpret basic types of graphs and charts.
- Self-assess their own performance at the end of each phase, as well as self-assessing their own final presentation.

In addition, students will be able to understand written input as well as produce written output related to the content objectives.

The module is designed to be undertaken in 4 or 5 hours, so the student workload should not be longer than this. According to the Common European Framework of Reference (CEFR), it is adapted to the B2 level (English) and will contribute to the development of the following skills: spoken comprehension, written comprehension and written production.

### 2.2.5.2. Learning outcomes

The *language skills (CEFR)* that are going to be dealt with in this module are the following:

1. Comprehension:
   a) Written:
      – Can understand the important information in simple, clearly drafted adverts in newspapers or magazines, provided that there are not too many abbreviations.
   b) Spoken:
      – Can understand straightforward factual information about common every day or job-related topics, identifying both general messages and specific details, provided that speech is clearly articulated in a generally familiar accent.
      – Can understand simple technical information, such as operating instructions for everyday equipment.
      – Can follow detailed directions.
      – Can understand recordings in the standard form of the language likely to be encountered in social, professional or academic life, and identify speaker viewpoints and attitudes as well as the information content.

2. Production:
   a) Written:
      – Can write straightforward, detailed descriptions on a range of familiar subjects within his/her field of interest.
      – Can write short, simple essays on topics of interest.

There are other skills, related to the contents of the module, that are also dealt with:

– Comparisons.
– Describing trends.

### 2.2.5.3. Contents: Phases and tasks

Table 14 summarises the activities to be carried out in the module.

**Table 14.** List of activities for module 4 ‘Reporting data’

| Phase | Aim | Tasks | Description | Time | Typology |
|---|---|---|---|---|---|
| Phase 1 | To provide an introduction on how to create graphs and the language that should be used to interpret them. | Task 1: video and questionnaire (I). | *Presentation task:* becoming familiar with graphs. | 20’ | Listening |
| | | Task 2: video and questionnaire (II). | *Presentation task:* learning to describe trends. | 20’ | Listening |
| | | Task 3: checklist | *Assessment task:* perception checklist. | 5’ | Reading |
| Phase 2 | To become familiar with graphs: learning the main types and the elements of graphs. | Task 4: working with different types of graphs. | *Practice task:* deciding which type of graph is the most appropriate to display the information provided. | 20’ | Reading |
| | | Task 5: identifying elements of a graph. | *Practice task:* identifying the information presented in several graphs. | 30’ | Reading and writing |
| | | Task 6: creating your own graph. | *Production task*: students create a graph from a table provided. | 30’-40’ | Writing |
| | | Task 7: checklist. | *Assessment task:* perception checklist. | 5’ | Reading |
| Phase 3 | To learn the language needed to describe trends (verbs, nouns, prepositions, etc.). | Task 8: verbs for describing trends. | *Practice task:* learning verbs to describe upward, downward, and stable trends. | 15’ | Writing |
| | | Task 9: nouns for describing trends. | *Practice task:* nominalising the verbs of task 8. | 15’ | Writing |
| | | Task 10: prepositions for describing trends. | *Practice task:* learning how to use prepositions when working with graphs. | 15’ | Reading and writing |
| | | Task 11: checklist. | *Assessment task:* perception checklist. | 5’ | Reading |

**Table 14.** Continued

| Phase | Aim | Tasks | Description | Time | Typology |
|---|---|---|---|---|---|
| Phase 4 | To gather all the information of the module to start describing trends. | Task 12: using the vocabulary learned. | *Practice task:* filling gapped statements with information from graphs. | 30' | Reading and writing |
| | | Task 13: linking graphs and statements. | *Practice task:* matching statements and graphs. | 20' | Reading |
| | | Task 14: interpreting a graph. | *Production task:* identifying the most relevant information in a given graph; writing a report. | 30'-45' | Writing |
| | | Task 15: checklist. | *Assessment task:* perception checklist. | 5' | Reading |

### *Phase 1: Warm-up phase*

The main learning goal of this phase is for students to become familiar with the basic aspects of a graph. This first step aims to provide the necessary knowledge about reporting trends. Students will explore some strategies for understanding the information provided in a graph and the language that should be used when describing them.

This phase will be completed in 45 minutes through three different tasks:

- Task 1 is in a presentation task for students to become familiar with graphs (listening activity).
- Task 2 is also a presentation task for students to learn how to describe trends (listening activity).
- Task 3 is a checklist to assess understanding (reading activity).

In the first presentation task (task 1), students will be asked to watch this module's first theoretical video about graphs, 'Video on Reporting Data I' (https://www.youtube.com/watch?v=iUKl44062OA) and answer a questionnaire comprising 6 multiple-choice questions.

In task 2, students will be asked to watch this module's second theoretical video about describing trends (https://www.youtube.com/watch?v=9CslIdoicYI&t=1s&ab_channel=LanguageEducationandResearchNetwork) and answer a questionnaire comprising 6 multiple-choice questions.

Finally, in task 3, students can assess their own learning by checking if they have properly understood the main ideas presented in the videos.

**Task 1. Questionnaire on the video I 'Becoming familiar with graphs'**

1. **What is a 'graph'?**
   a. A diagram that shows the relation between two variables.
   b. A variable measured.
   c. The starting point for other productions.
   d. An arrangement of data in rows and columns.
2. **Which one of these is NOT a type of graph?**
   a. Bar graph.
   b. Figure graph.
   c. Circle graph.
   d. Histogram.
3. **Which type of graph allows part-to-whole comparisons and comparisons across categories?**
   a. Histogram.
   b. Line graph.
   c. Stacked bar graph.
   d. Bar graph.
4. **What type of graph is represented in the picture (Figure 8)?**
   a. Histogram.
   b. Line graph.
   c. Bar graph.
   d. Circle graph.

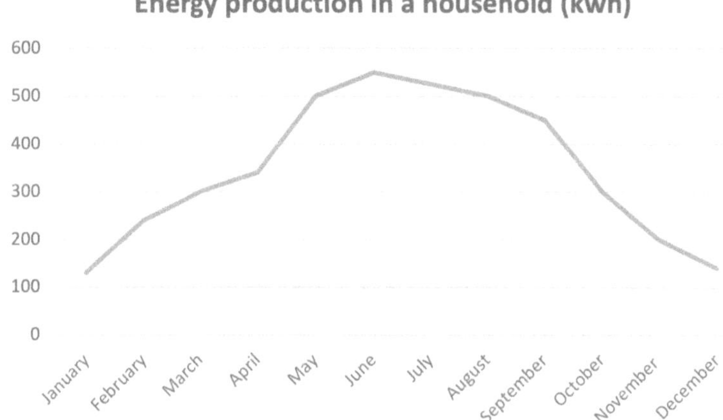


**Figure 8.** Example of graph. Source: Own elaboration

5. **Which one of these is NOT a compulsory element of a graph?**
   a. Title of the axis.
   b. Legend.
   c. Quotation.
   d. Data table.
6. **Which of these elements provides an explanation for the colour code?**
   a. Title of the 'y axis'.
   b. Quotation.
   c. Dimension.
   d. Legend.

**Task 2. Questionnaire on the video II 'Learning how to describe trends'**

1. **Which of these is NOT an element for trend descriptions?**
   a. Graphs.
   b. Change.
   c. Place and time.
   d. Speed of change.
2. **Which one of these is NOT a way of indicating the amount of change in a trend?**
   a. Analysing whether it is an up or down trend.
   b. Indicating the initial and final value of the variable.
   c. Describing the change with the help of adverbs.
   d. Indicating the amount of variation.
3. **Which is a good way of describing up and down trends?**
   a. Using reporting verbs.
   b. Using signpost language.
   c. Using metaphors.
   d. None of the above.
4. **The verb 'to level off' refers to**...
   a. An up trend.
   b. A stable trend.
   c. A down trend.
   d. None of the above.
5. **Which of these adverbs represents the least significant change in the trend?**
   a. Vastly.
   b. Dramatically.
   c. Hugely.
   d. Considerably.
6. **This is part of a description of a graph: 'the diagram reaches a peak of 11 % in 2010, and the minimum of 4 % in 2018.' What is its purpose?**
   a. To show the compulsory elements in the graph.
   b. To describe the graph's general impression.

c. To report slight differences and changes.
d. To report the maximum and minimum values.

**Task 3. Checklist**

1. **I have learnt what a graph is**
   a. Yes.
   b. No.
2. **I know the main types and elements of graphs.**
   a. Yes.
   b. No.
3. **I can distinguish between up, down and stable trends.**
   a. Yes.
   b. No.
4. **I know the steps to follow to describe a trend.**
   a. Yes.
   b. No.

***Phase 2: Getting used to graphs***

The main aim of this phase is to work with the most relevant information about graphs: the main types of graphs and the elements that each graph should include so that students can create their own graph.

This phase will be completed in one hour and a half through four different tasks:

- Task 4 is a practice task for students to work with different types of graphs (reading activity).
- Task 5 is also a practice task for students to identify the elements of a graph (reading and writing activity).
- Task 6 is a production task for students to create their own graph (writing activity).
- Task 7 is a checklist to assess understanding (reading activity).

In the first practice task (task 4), learners will have to decide which type of graph (line, circle, histogram, bar or stacked bar graph) is the most appropriate to display information provided in a series of tables. To carry out this task, students will work with the materials 'Tables and graphs'.

In the second practice task (task 5), students will identify the information presented in several graphs, labelling the different elements they can find, using the materials presented in 'Unlabelled graphs'.

In the production task (task 6), students will create their own graph in Excel from a table provided in the materials 'Data for the graph', which represents the surface of marine sites.

Finally, in task 7, students can assess their own learning, checking if they have properly understood the contents of the phase.

### Task 4. Working with different types of graphs

*As you know, there are different types of graphs. Look at Figure 9 and decide which type of graph is the most appropriate to display the information on the tables below. In some tables, several options are possible.*

| Materials for Task 4. 'Working with different types of graphs' |
|---|

- **Types of graphs:**

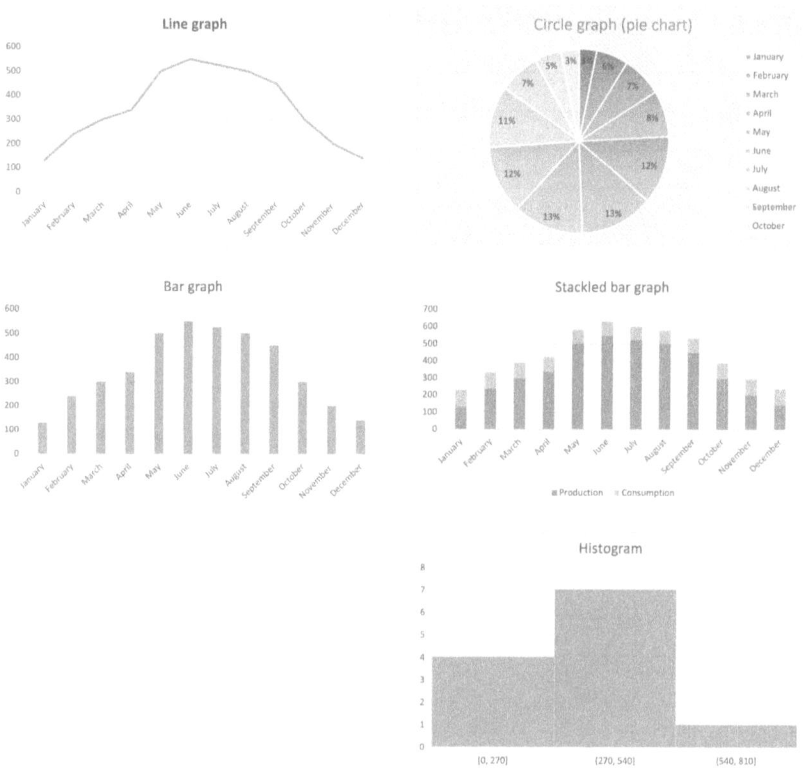


**Figure 9.** Types of graphs. Source: Own elaboration

- **Tables**

**1)**

| **Years** | **Agricultural emissions (%)** |
|---|---|
| **2005** | 9.2 |
| **2006** | 8.5 |
| **2007** | 8.2 |
| **2008** | 11.3 |
| **2009** | 17.9 |
| **2010** | 19.9 |
| **2011** | 21.4 |

| Years | Agricultural emissions (%) |
|---|---|
| **2012** | 24.8 |
| **2013** | 26.1 |
| **2014** | 24.5 |
| **2015** | 22.1 |
| **2016** | 19.6 |
| **2017** | 17.2 |
| **2018** | 15.3 |

**2)**

| Province | Land use emissions (%) |
|---|---|
| **Badajoz** | 42.8 |
| **Cáceres** | 57.2 |

**3)**

| EU countries | GHG footprint of consumption |
|---|---|
| **Austria** | 127 |
| **Belgium** | 117 |
| **Bulgaria** | 51 |
| **Croatia** | 63 |
| **Cyprus** | 89 |
| **Czechia** | 91 |
| **Denmark** | 128 |
| **Estonia** | 82 |
| **Finland** | 111 |
| **France** | 104 |
| **Germany** | 122 |
| **Greece** | 68 |
| **Hungary** | 71 |
| **Ireland** | 189 |
| **Italy** | 96 |
| **Latvia** | 69 |
| **Lithuania** | 80 |

| EU countries | GHG footprint of consumption |
|---|---|
| **Luxembourg** | 261 |
| **Malta** | 98 |
| **Netherlands** | 129 |
| **Poland** | 70 |
| **Portugal** | 77 |
| **Romania** | 65 |
| **Slovakia** | 73 |
| **Slovenia** | 87 |
| **Spain** | 91 |
| **Sweden** | 120 |
| **United Kingdom** | 105 |

**4)**

| Energy carriers | Spain | Germany | Hungary |
|---|---|---|---|
| Total petroleum products | 47 | 35 | 29 |
| Natural gas | 20 | 23 | 32 |
| Solid fossil fuels | 9 | 23 | 9 |
| Nuclear energy | 11 | 6 | 15 |
| Renewable energy | 12 | 13 | 11 |
| Other | 1 | 0 | 4 |
| ***Total*** | ***100*** | ***100*** | ***100*** |

**5)**

| Household final energy consumption | Number of EU countries |
|---|---|
| <10,000 | 1 |
| [10,000–20,000] | 11 |
| [20,000–30,000] | 5 |
| [30,000–40,000] | 2 |
| [40,000–50,000] | 6 |
| >50,000 | 3 |

**Source: Own elaboration with data from Eurostat (https://ec.europa.eu/eurostat)**

## Task 5. Identifying the elements of a graph

*Identify the information presented in the graphs below (see Figures 10, 11 and 12). Once you have identified the elements, label them:*

- *Title of the diagram.*
- *Information about time and place.*
- *Legend.*
- *Title of the y axis.*
- *Title of the x axis.*
- *Dimension of the variables.*
- *Quotation.*

*However, in some of these graphs some elements are missing. Can you find the information that is missing in each of them? Why do you think there is information missing?*

*Once you have finished, you may check your answers with the ones provided in figures 22, 23 and 24 in the answer key.*

| Materials for Task 5. 'Identifying the elements of a graph' |
|---|

- **Graph 1**

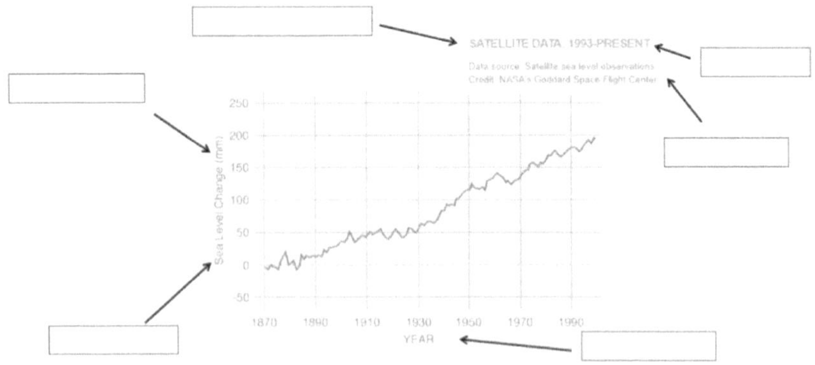


**Figure 10.** Unlabelled graph 1. Source: https://climate.nasa.gov/vital-signs/sea-level/ (Retrieved 01/01/2021)

- **Graph 2**

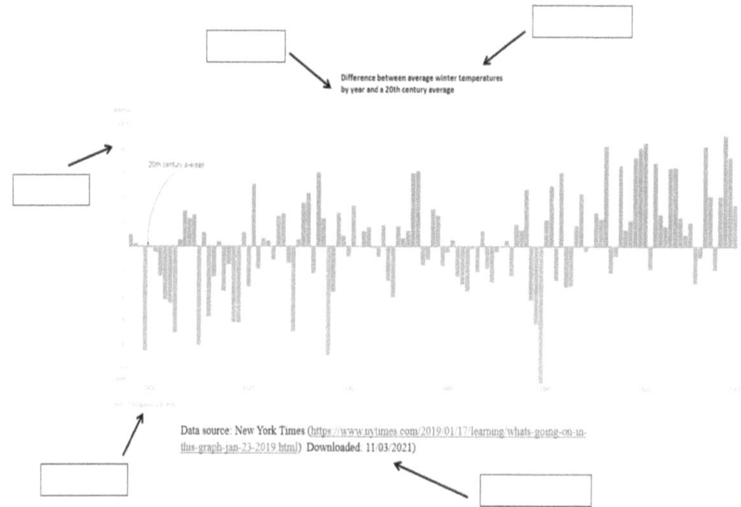


**Figure 11.** Unlabelled graph 2. Source: https://www.nytimes.com/2019/01/17/learning/whats-going-on-in-this-graph-jan-23-2019.html (Retrieved 11/03/2021)

- **Graph 3**

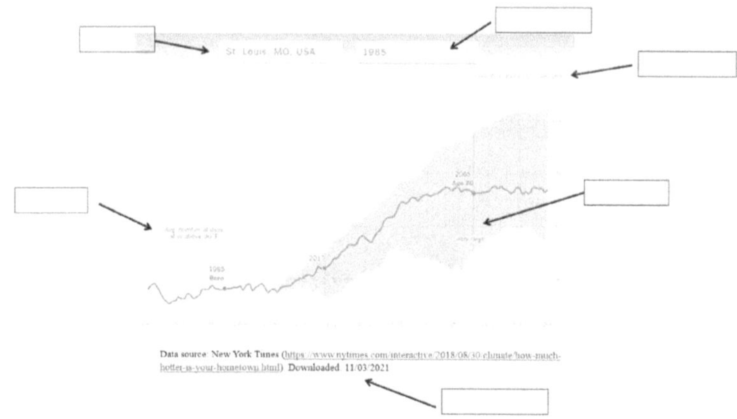


**Figure 12.** Unlabelled graph 3. Source: https://www.nytimes.com/interactive/2018/08/30/climate/how-much-hotter-is-your-hometown.html. (Retrieved: 11/03/2021)

## Task 6. Creating your own graph

*Now that you are familiar with graphs, it is time to create your own from the information in the table. To do this, you can use Microsoft Excel or a similar type of spreadsheet programme.*

*The table below represents the surface of marine sites designated under Natura 2000 in the European Union, from 2011 to 2019. When your graph is ready, you may like to compare it with the one provided as a model answer in figure 25 in the answer key.*

Materials for Task 6. 'Creating your own graph'

- **Table**

| **Year** | **Marine protected area (km$^2$)** |
|---|---|
| 2013 | 177483 |
| 2014 | 244054 |
| 2015 | 286145 |
| 2016 | 308364 |
| 2017 | 402552 |
| 2018 | 419769 |
| 2019 | 441001 |

Source of data: European Environment Agency (EEA), European Commission - Directorate-General for Environment (DG ENV)

## Task 7. Checklist

1. **I can distinguish the main elements of a graph.**
   a. Yes.
   b. No.
2. **I can describe a graph.**
   a. Yes.
   b. No.
3. **I am able to create my own graph.**
   a. Yes.
   b. No.

***Phase 3: Vocabulary to describe trends***

The main learning aim of this phase is for students to become familiar with the language needed to describe trends, so they will work with verbs, nouns, prepositions and adverbs.

The duration of this phase will be between 45 minutes and 1 hour, and it will be completed through four different tasks:

- Task 8 is a practice task for students to classify verbs for describing trends (reading and writing activity).
- Task 9 is a practice task for students to learn about nouns for describing trends (reading and writing activity).
- Task 10 is a practice task for students to learn about prepositions for describing trends (reading and writing activity).
- Task 11 is a checklist to assess understanding (reading activity).

In the first practice task (task 8), students will classify a list of verbs (in the materials 'Verbs for describing trends') depending on their purpose in describing a trend.

In task 9, learners will guess the nouns for the verbs used (provided in the materials 'Nouns for describing trends') when describing trends.

In task 10, students will learn and practice key prepositions (provided in the materials 'Prepositions for describing trends'), focusing on their use in describing charts and diagrams. Next, they will complete gapped sentences using prepositions.

Finally, in the assessment task (task 11), students can assess their own learning, checking if they have properly understood the contents of the phase.

**Task 8. Verbs for describing trends**

*Once you have practiced with the elements and types of graphs, it is time to learn how to analyse them. This first task is a vocabulary task. Here, you will learn how to express three trends: when the graph goes down, when it goes up and when it remains stable.*

*Classify the words from the following list according to their meaning. Remember that more is up ↑, less is down ↓ and → is stability.*

Materials for Task 8. 'Verbs for describing trends'

- Increase
- Fluctuate
- Decrease
- Go up
- Go down
- Vary
- Fall
- Stabilise
- Stay the same
- Grow
- Decline
- Boom
- Climb
- Jump
- Level out
- Collapse
- Expand

| | | | | | | |
|---|---|---|---|---|---|---|
| ↑ | | | | | | |
| ↓ | | | | | | |
| → | | | | | | |

## Task 9. Nouns for describing trends

*So far, we have been using verbs to talk about trends. However, we can also talk about trends using nouns, most of them related to the verbs used above.*

*Let's see if you can guess the nouns in this table. We have done the first one for you as an example.*

Materials for Task 9. Nouns for describing trends

| **Upward trend** | **Verb** | **Noun** |
|---|---|---|
| | To rise | A rise |
| | To increase | |
| | To grow | |
| | To climb | |
| | To boom | |
| | To improve | |
| | To recover | |
| | To expand | |
| **Downward trend** | To fall | |
| | To decrease | |
| | To decline | |
| | To drop | |
| | To collapse | |
| | To reduce | |
| | To deteriorate | |
| | To weaken | |
| **Stability** | To level out | |
| | To stay the same | |
| | To stabilize | |
| | To fluctuate | |
| | To vary | |
| | To peak | |
| | To be volatile | |
| | To be/remain flat | |

## Task 10. Prepositions for describing trends

In this activity, you will learn and practice key prepositions, focusing on their use in describing charts and diagrams.

In the first part of the task, you are presented with examples of prepositions and their use.

Once you have analysed how prepositions are used, you will be asked to fill in the gaps in several sentences, using prepositions.

## Materials for Task 10. 'Prepositions for describing trends'

**1. Study the following examples of prepositions and their use:**

- There was a fall **in** $CO_2$ levels...
- We can expect a five percent increase **in** greenhouse gas emissions.
- **In** mid-April the ice caps...
- Gas prices rose **in** June .../Gas prices kept rising **throughout/during** June ...
- This was followed **by** ...
- ... the figures were characterized **by** a number of peaks.
- ... the rates have risen **by** two percentage points.
- Our contamination is up **by** 36 percent.
- It increased **by** 20 %... /There was an increase **of** 5 % ...
- The results have improved **by** an average **of** eight percent.
- **Over** the last few months, the pollution has advanced again,
- **Over** the period **from** ... **to** ...,
- The plastic consuming was up and was close **to** reaching a high again,
- ... the percentage **of** ...
- The percentage **of** green options continues to increase.
- These figures are expressed **as** a percentage **of** the total.
- 20 percent **of** the respondents.
- the values fluctuated **around/at** this level ...
- Last year started **on** a positive note,

**2. Let's practice: Fill in the gaps in the sentences below with one word.**

1. What percentage ___ water is affected ___ contamination?
2. Pollution rates have risen ___ two percentage points.
3. The percentage ___ nuclear energy facilities continues ___ increase.
4. Farmers only recovered a very small percentage ___ land.
5. What percentage ___ green energy sources is used?
6. Average CO2 emissions per km have risen ___ two percentage points.
7. These figures are expressed ___ a percentage ___ the total.
8. Only 40 percent ___ people bothered to recycle last year.
9. They discovered a 10 percent fall ___ industrial waste.
10. _____ the last years, footprints of consumption fluctuated _____ 20 points.

**Task 11. Checklist**

1. **I am able to use verbs and nouns to describe trends.**
   a. Yes.
   b. No.
2. **I can use prepositions to describe trends.**
   a. Yes.
   b. No.
3. **I can distinguish upward and downward changes and stability in a trend.**
   a. Yes.
   b. No.

### *Phase 4: Describing trends*

The main learning aim of this phase is for students to start describing trends on their own. Students will put into practice the vocabulary learned in the previous tasks to describe a graph without guidance or support.

Phase 4 will be completed in one hour and a half through four different tasks:

- Task 12 is a practice task for students to use the vocabulary learned (reading and writing activity).
- Task 13 is also a practice task for students to link graphs and statements (reading activity).
- Task 14 is a production task to analyse the general information a graph provides (writing activity).
- Task 15 is also a production task for students to interpret a graph (writing activity).
- Task 16 is a checklist to assess understanding (reading activity).

In the first practice task (task 12), students will use the vocabulary of the module to fill in the gaps in several statements. These statements are descriptions of graphs provided in the materials 'Using the vocabulary learned'.

In task 13, learners will match graphs with statements, focusing on the information in the graphs. To carry out this task, students will use the materials 'Linking graphs and statements'.

In the first production task (task 14), students will analyse the general characteristics of a graph and provide an overall description, using the materials 'How to organise a trend description'.

In task 15, students will have to analyse a graph (provided in the materials 'Interpreting a graph') that shows the evolution of Arctic ice caps since the year 1980. They are expected to identify the main elements of the graphs and label them, as well as writing a report to describe the most relevant information the graph provides.

Finally, in task 14, students can assess their own learning, checking if they have properly understood the contents of the phase.

## Task 12. Using the vocabulary learned

*Read paragraphs (A – C) below; each graph (please look at Figures 13, 14 and 15) is followed by a gapped text. Fill in the gaps using the words in the table below each graph.*

| Materials for Task 12. 'Using the vocabulary learned' |
| --- |

A) The graph shows greenhouse gas emissions in the European Union between 2009 and 2018

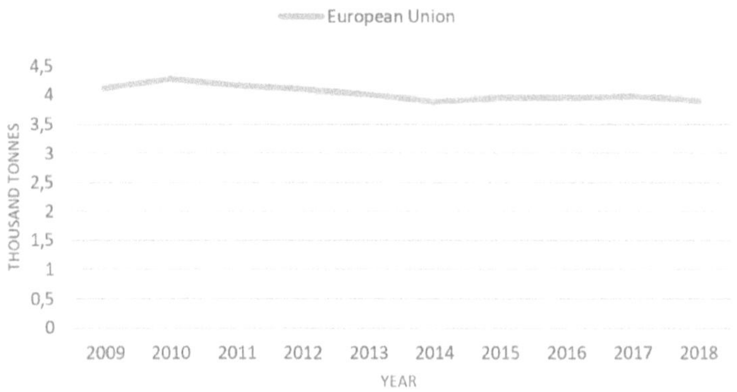


**Figure 13.** Labelled graph 1. Source https://ec.europa.eu/eurostat/web/main/eurostat/web/main/help/faq/data-services. (Retrieved 17/03/2021)

| Rose | Decrease | stable | reaching | Slight |
|---|---|---|---|---|

In general, the emission rate is relatively_______. In 2010, the emissions_______. However, in 2014 there is a _______ _______, _______ less than 4 m thousand tons of gas emissions.

B) This graph shows the consumption of ozone-depleting substances (ODS) in tons from 1986 to 2019 in the European Union (EU) and globally. The analysis below is from the EU rate.

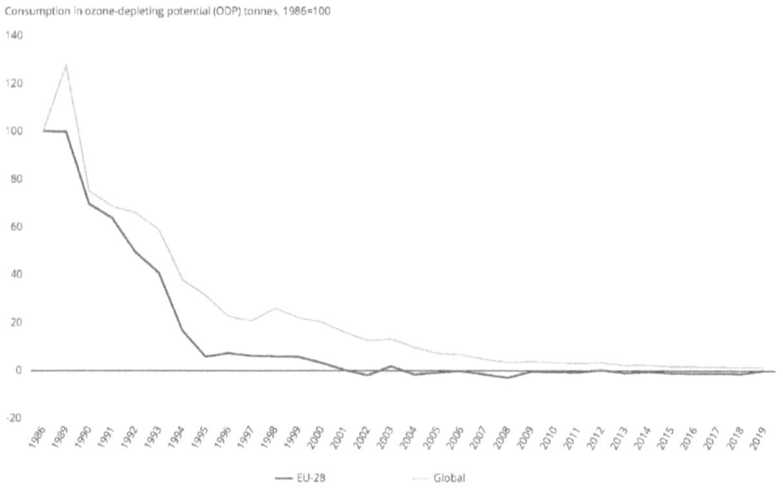


**Figure 14.** Labelled graph 2. Source https://ec.europa.eu/eurostat/web/main/eurostat/web/main/help/faq/data-services. (Retrieved 17/03/2021)

| levelled out | Fall | Remaining | Drastically | dropped flat |
|---|---|---|---|---|

After _______ _______ in 100 tonnes of ODS from 1986 to 1989, the ozone substances ratio _______ _______ to around 10 tonnes in 2009. The ratio continued to __ _____ until 2008. Since then, the rate has_______.

C) This graph shows the percentage of final energy consumption in households by fuel in the European Union (EU) and Euro area (EA) from 1990 to 2018.

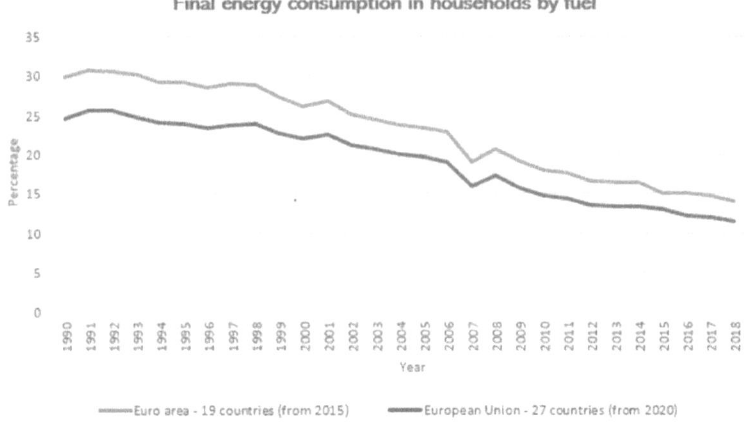


**Figure 15.** Labelled graph 3. Source https://ec.europa.eu/eurostat/web/main/eurostat/web/main/help/faq/data-services. (Retrieved 17/03/2021)

| went down | peak | stable | decrease | continuously gradual |
|---|---|---|---|---|

After being relatively _______ at around 30 % (EU) and 25 % (EA) between 1990 and 1998, the consumption of fuel experienced a _______ _______ until 2007, when it attained a _______ of 19 % (EU) and 16 % (EA). Since then, both rates _______ _______ to _______ 16 % (EU) and 12 % (EA).

## Task 13. Linking graphs and statements

Match the statements (A – F) with graphs (1 – 6), in Figure 16

| Materials for Task 13. 'Linking graphs and statements' |
|---|

- **Statements**

A. GHG footprint of consumption rate climbed steadily but flattened off to a rate of around 2.6 %.
B. GHG footprint of consumption rate grew rapidly over the first two years, then quickly dropped.
C. Ozone substances ratio reached a peak in 2015; since then it has remained stable.
D. Plastic contamination in oceans rate dropped by more than 4 percent point in 2009 and then again slightly in 2012.

E. Renewable energy used rate steadily decreased to 1.1 % in 2016 and after that increased to 1.4 % in 2018.
F. Transport pollution rate slightly increased from 75 % to 79 %.

- **Graphs**

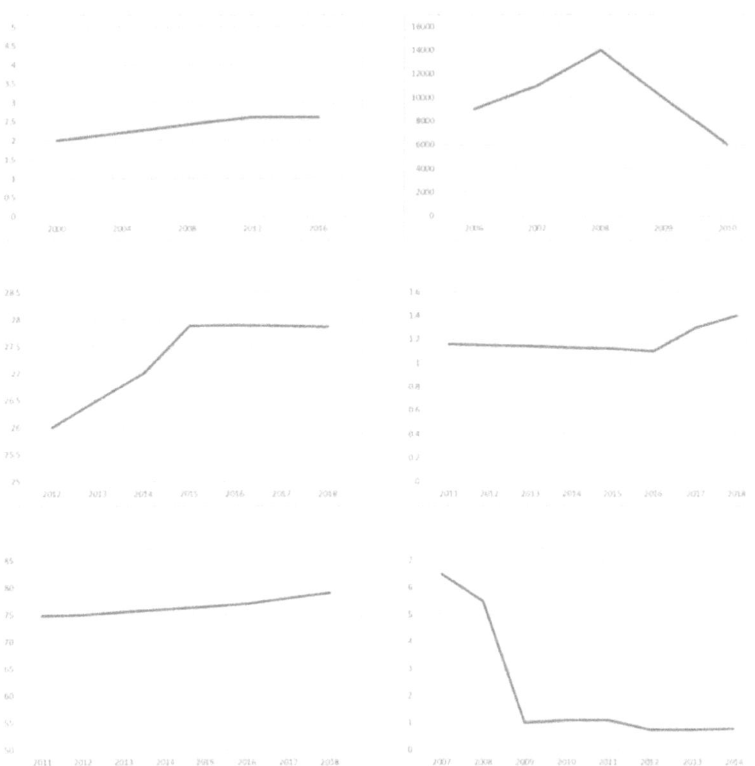

**Figure 16.** Graphs to match with statements. Source: Own elaboration with data from Eurostat (https://ec.europa.eu/eurostat)

## Task 14. How to organise a trend description

*In this task, you will have to analyse the graph below (please, look at Figure 17). Specify:*

- *The overall description of the graph: What are you describing? When? What about the source?*
- *Maximum and minimum values.*
- *Detailed description of the trend.*

| Materials for Task 14. 'How to organise a trend description' |
|---|

**Figure 17.** Graph for description. Source: https://fred.stlouisfed.org/ (Retrieved 22/03/2021)

## Task 15. Interpreting a graph

*The graph below (Figure 18) shows the evolution of Arctic ice caps since the year 1980. Identify the most relevant information and write a report describing it. You will have to:*

1. *Identify the main elements of the graph.*
2. *Write a short description of the graph (general impression, maximum and minimum, changes, etc.) Remember to include the five basic elements for trend discussion (change; variable; amount and speed of change; place; time).*

You can check your answers with the ones provided in figure 26 and the short description included as a model answer for this task in the answer key.

Materials for Task 15. 'Interpreting a graph'

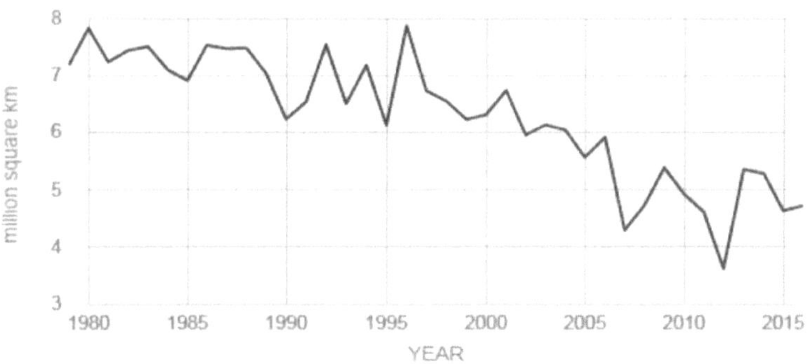


**Figure 18.** Graph for description. Source: https://climate.nasa.gov/vital-signs/arctic-sea-ice/ (Retrieved 11/02/2021)

## Task 16. Checklist

1. **I can use the vocabulary of the module to describe trends.**
   a. Yes.
   b. No.
2. **I can match descriptions with graphs.**
   a. Yes.
   b. No.
3. **I am able to describe a graph without guidance or support.**
   a. Yes.
   b. No.

Table 15 shows a rubric that has been developed to assess this module and that can be used as a self-assessment, peer-assessment tool for students as well as an evaluation tool for instructors if the module is taught in a class.

*External sources for materials and tasks*

- https://ec.europa.eu/eurostat
- https://www.nytimes.com/2019/01/17/learning/whats-going-on-in-this-graph-jan-23-2019.html

- https://climate.nasa.gov/vital-signs/sea-level/
- https://www.nytimes.com/interactive/2018/08/30/climate/how-much-hotter-is-your-hometown.html
- https://ec.europa.eu/eurostat/statistics-explained/index.php?title=File:Surface_of_marine_sites_designated_under_Natura_2000,_EU-27,_2013-2019_(km%C2%B2)_update.png
- https://appsso.eurostat.ec.europa.eu/nui/show.do?dataset=env_air_gge&lang=en
- https://www.eea.europa.eu/data-and-maps/figures/consumption-of-controlled-ozone-depleting
- https://ec.europa.eu/eurostat/en/web/products-datasets/-/T2020_RK210
- https://fred.stlouisfed.org/
- https://climate.nasa.gov/vital-signs/arctic-sea-ice/

## 2.2.5.4. Rubric for assessment

**Table 15.** Rubric to assess module 4 'Reporting data'

| Element | Excellent (4) | Good (3) | Fair (2) | Poor (1) |
|---|---|---|---|---|
| **Content Elements** | | | | |
| Required elements in a graph | The graph includes all the required elements: title of the diagram, time, place, legend, title of X axis, title of Y axis, quotation, and dimension. | The graph includes at least 6 of the required elements. | The student mixes up the different elements in the graph, but more than 4 of the required elements are included. | Less than 4 of the required elements in a graph are included. |
| Types of graphs | **Excellent (4)** | | **Poor (1)** | |
| | The student is able to distinguish between the main types of graphs: line graphs, bar graphs, histograms, circle graphs, stacked-bar graphs and to choose the most suitable one for the task. | | The type of graph chosen is not most appropriate for the task. | |
| **Element** | **Excellent (4)** | **Good (3)** | **Fair (2)** | **Poor (1)** |
| **Language Elements** | | | | |
| Vocabulary | The student uses a wide variety of vocabulary to express change (up, down, stable trends) and amount of change (very intense, intense change and significant change), using different verbs, nouns and adverbs. | The student uses a fair variety of vocabulary to express change and amount of change, using different verbs, nouns and adverbs. | Vocabulary to express change and amount of change is barely used. The student uses some verbs, nouns and adverbs, but repeats some of them. | The student does not use the specific vocabulary to express change and amount of change. |
| Language for describing trends/ organization of the information | The description of the graph has a clear guiding thread. The student includes general information about the graph (variables explored, source. . .), reports the maximum and the minimum, and describes all the changes (amount of change, speed of change, place and time) in the trend. | The description of the graph has a guiding thread. The student includes at least 2 of the required elements, and the description of the trend is mostly accurate. | The description of the graph has a guiding thread. The student describes the trend but in a rather vague way. | Information is not organised in a straightforward thread. It only includes one of the required elements for reporting data, and the trend in the graph is barely described. |

### 2.2.6. Module 5: The language of presentations

#### 2.2.6.1. Overview and aims

This module aims to provide students with the fundamental knowledge and tools to create and deliver presentations. Being able to express oneself clearly and convincingly is a skill needed in all kinds of situations. Therefore, gaining practice at university is very important and will help students prepare for their future job. Presentations are commonly used as a part of the oral work conducted by students in their different subjects at university, and, in most degree and master programmes, students need to present a final dissertation to finalise their studies.

This topic will be introduced through five different self-study and online task phases, incorporating both theoretical aspects and practical exercises under the principles of self-study and self-assessment. In short, the goal of this module is to provide the knowledge necessary to understand and write a presentation, focusing specifically on the language structures (signpost language).

The interactive version of the module developed in *Genial.ly* can be accessed here: https://view.genial.ly/5ffd6ec236185d5bd50d1eec/learning-experience-didactic-unit-the-language-of-presentationsmodule

And the introductory video hosted in our *L2EARN* channel in YouTube is also freely available: https://www.youtube.com/watch?v=g7i3I6wyhIU

At the end of this module, students will be able to:

- Create their own presentation without any type of guidance or support.
- Divide their presentation into phases, linking these with appropriate language structures.
- Self-assess their own performance at the end of each phase, as well as self-assessing their own final presentation.

In addition, students will be able to understand written input as well as produce written output related to the content objectives. They will also be provided with language activities to reinforce the knowledge and use of signpost language in context.

This module is designed to be completed in 5 or 6 hours, so student workload should not be longer than this. According to the Common European Framework of Reference (CEFR), it is adapted to B2 level (English), and will contribute to the development of the following skills: spoken comprehension, written comprehension and written production.

### 2.2.6.2. Learning outcomes

The *language skills (CEFR)* that are going to be dealt with in this module are the following:

1. Comprehension:
   a) Written:
      - Can scan quickly through long and complex texts, locating relevant details.
      - Can obtain information, ideas and opinions from highly specialised sources within his/her field.
      - Can recognise when a text provides factual information and when it seeks to convince readers of something.

   b) Spoken:
      - Can follow extended speech and complex lines of argument provided the topic is reasonably familiar, and the direction of the talk is sign-posted by explicit markers.
      - Can understand recordings in the standard form of the language likely to be encountered in social, professional or academic life and identify speaker viewpoints and attitudes as well as content information.

2. Production:
   a) Written:
      - Can write an essay or report that develops an argument systematically with appropriate highlighting of significant points and relevant supporting detail.
      - Can, in preparing for a potentially complicated or awkward situation, plan what to say in the event of

different reactions, reflecting on what expression would be appropriate.
- Can plan what is to be said and the means to say it, considering the effect on the recipient(s).

b) Spoken:

- Can give a clear, systematically developed presentation, with highlighting of significant points, and relevant supporting detail.
- Can depart spontaneously from a prepared text and follow up interesting points raised by members of the audience, often showing remarkable fluency and ease of expression.
- Can give a clear, prepared presentation, giving reasons in support of or against a particular point of view, discussing the advantages and disadvantages of various options.
- Can answer follow up questions with a degree of fluency and spontaneity which pose no strain for either him/herself or the audience.
- Can give clear, systematically developed descriptions and presentations, with appropriate highlighting of significant points, and relevant supporting detail.

The main *language function* developed in this module is:

- Delivering an oral presentation.

### 2.2.6.3. Contents: Phases and tasks

Table 16 summarises the activities that are developed in the module.

**Table 16.** List of activities for module 5 'The language of presentations'

| Phase | Aim | Tasks | Description | Time | Typology |
|---|---|---|---|---|---|
| Phase 1 | To give an introduction on how to create a presentation and the language that should be included. | Task 1: video and questionnaire. | *Presentation task*: video and questionnaire. understanding presentations | 30' | Listening |
| | | Task 2: checklist | *Assessment task*: perception checklist. | 5' | Reading |
| Phase 2 | To provide the basic tools to organise a presentation. Students will become familiar with the main parts and characteristics of presentations and the language used to introduce each of the parts. | Task 3: how to organise a presentation | *Practice task*: organising different extracts of a presentation. | 40' | Reading |
| | | Task 4: checklist | *Assessment task*: perception checklist. | 5' | Reading |
| Phase 3 | To focus on the language structures used in the introduction and conclusion, providing key language tips and discursive skills to create a good presentation. | Task 5: writing an introduction | *Practice task:* changing signpost language phrases related to the introduction. | 30'-40' | Reading and writing |
| | | Task 6: handling difficult situations | *Practice task*: learning how to act when answering questions on presentations. | 30'-40' | Reading and writing |
| | | Task 7: checklist | *Assessment task*: perception checklist. | 5' | Reading |
| Phase 4 | To provide learners with some tips to capture and highlight the essential information the audience needs to understand a presentation. | Task 8: identifying signpost language | *Practice task:* identifying signpost language in a video. | 30' | Listening |
| | | Task 9: checklist | *Assessment task*: perception checklist. | 5' | Reading |

(*Continued*)

**Table 16.** Continued

| Phase | Aim | Tasks | Description | Time | Typology |
|---|---|---|---|---|---|
| Phase 5 | To assess students' ability to create their own presentation (without guidance and support). | Task 10: creating your own presentation | *Production task*: writing, recording and assessing their own original presentation. | 90'-120' | Writing |
| | | Task 11: checklist | *Assessment task*: perception checklist. | 5' | Reading |

### *Phase 1: Warm-up*

The main learning aim of this phase is for students to become familiar with the basic aspects of a presentation. This first step aims to provide the necessary knowledge about understanding and developing presentations as well as identifying their key elements. Students will explore some strategies for understanding presentations and signpost language.

Phase 1 will be completed in 30 minutes through two different tasks:

– Task 1 is a presentation task for students to understand and make presentations (listening activity).
– Task 2 is a checklist to assess understanding (reading activity).

In the presentation task (task 1), students will be asked to watch this module's theoretical video about presentations, 'The language of presentations' (https://www.youtube.com/watch?v=g7i3I6wyhIU&ab_channel=LanguageEducationandResearchNetwork) and answer a questionnaire comprising 10 multiple-choice questions. This is the first time the concept of presentations is introduced.

In task 2, students can assess their own learning, checking if they have properly understood the main ideas presented in the video.

#### **Task 1. Questionnaire on the theoretical video**

1. **What is a 'presentation'?**
   a. A means of communication that can be adapted to various speaking situations.

b. A short piece of writing by a student on a particular subject.
c. A piece of writing about a particular subject that is published in a newspaper or magazine.
d. A spoken or written account that gives information about a particular subject, situation, or event.

2. **Which aspects should be carefully considered when giving a presentation?**
    a. Persuasion, explanation, or clarification.
    b. Body paragraphs.
    c. Step-by-step preparation, methodology, language and means of presenting the information.
    d. It should include direct quotes.
3. **What is 'signpost language'?**
    a. It refers to the words and phrases that people use to tell the listener what has just happened, and what is going to happen next, guiding the listener through the presentation.
    b. It refers to the oral, written, auditory, and visual language proficiency required to learn effectively in schools and academic programmes.
    c. A language primarily developed to disguise conversation, originally because of a criminal enterprise, though the term is also used loosely to refer to informal jargon.
    d. The linguistic style used for casual communication.
4. **Why are visual aids important in presentations?**
    a. They are useful for learning new vocabulary, spelling, and pronunciation.
    b. They provide a first impression.
    c. They inspire your audience and leave them with positive feelings about thespeaker.
    d. Visual aids help to follow your spoken presentation and keep the audience's attention.
5. **What is signpost language similar to?**
    a. Lecture cues (what lecturers use).
    b. Formulaic language (verbal expressions that are fixed in form, used in academic contexts).
    c. Both of the above.

6. **According to the video, which type of phrases should you learn more about?**
   a. Phrases for introducing the topic.
   b. Phrases for visual aids and transitions.
   c. Phrases for stating the purpose.
   d. All the above answers are correct.
7. **Which phrase is used for giving the structure of your presentation?**
   a. My aim today is. . .
   b. Good morning, ladies and gentlemen.
   c. This talk is divided into three main parts.
8. **Which phrase is used for showing visual aids?**
   a. If we look at this slide. . .
   b. My presentation will last about x minutes.
   c. Look!
9. **Why are transition structures so important?**
   a. Because of the differences between listening and reading, it is not easy to know where a section starts or ends.
   b. Because a presentation needs to be structured, and they are the best way of doing so.
   c. Neither of the above.
10. **What should you do in your conclusion?**
   a. Sum up the main points, finish, close and invite questions.
   b. Sum up the main points, conclude, close and invite questions.
   c. Thank the audience, sum up the main points and close.

**Task 2. Checklist phase 1**

1. **I have watched the video on 'The language of presentations'.**
   a. Yes.
   b. No.
2. **I have answered all the questions correctly.**
   a. Yes.
   b. No.

3. **I have learned about the definition and key elements of a presentation.**
   a. Yes.
   b. No.

### *Phase 2: Organising a presentation*

The main aim of phase 2 is to provide students with the basic tools to organise a presentation. Students will identify the main parts and characteristics of presentations and the language used to introduce each of the parts.

Phase 2 will be completed in 45 minutes through two different tasks:

- Task 3 is a practice task for students to learn how to organise a presentation (reading activity).
- Task 4 is a checklist to assess understanding (reading activity).

In task 3, students will order several extracts of a presentation (provided in the material 'How to organise a presentation') so that the presentation makes sense. They should find out which extract corresponds to each part of the presentation by focusing on the language structures used.

In task 4, students can assess their own learning, checking if they have properly understood the contents of the phase.

### Task 3. How to organise a presentation

*The following extracts are part of a presentation script:*

- *Can you put them in order so that the presentation makes sense?*
- *Highlight the part of the presentation to which each box would belong.*

## Materials for Task 3. 'How to organise a presentation'

**Extract** . . .

Let's recap. The most important points we have covered in this presentation are the following (. . .).

There are some interesting websites and blogs where you will also find some complementary information and interactive resources.

Are there any questions? Many thanks for your attention and I really hope that you consider bringing real children's literature into your classroom.

**Extract** . . .

So now that you know HOW to do it, you just need to select some suitable children's book for your pupils. Some of the best-known and most acclaimed writers are Julia Donaldson (you are surely familiar with 'The Gruffalo'), Eric Carle (everybody knows 'The very hungry caterpillar') or Maurice Sendak and his unique story 'Where the wild things are'.

**Extract** . . .

Hello, my name is __________ I am studying a degree in Education and, today, I am going to talk about the benefits of reading for school children. You may have never thought about this topic but over the next 30 minutes or so you will learn some tips to introduce children's literature in your classrooms and I am quite sure that you will find it very interesting. The main aspects I will be covering in this presentation are the following:

First, I will explain the reasons why 'real' reading needs 'real' books. Then, I will illustrate how to use children's book in the classroom. And, finally, we will have a look at some of the most popular books for children and talk about their authors.

So, how many of you have used or have thought about using children's book in their classrooms? Please raise your hand if the answer is yes. Ok, so some of you have.

**Extract . . .**

If you really want to make the most of this practice, you need to plan how to do it considering aspects such as: Should I use real books or reading books? How many books do I need?

If you have ever thought about these questions, it's time you bring children's books into your classroom!

**Extract . . .**

It is important for you to understand that this is a beneficial practice for the kids. In a substantial body of research, scholars have documented the multiple benefits of using children's literature in classrooms. They conclude that literature not only assists children to learn to read but also helps them develop an appreciation for reading as a pleasurable aesthetic experience.

Going back to our previous questions:

1. Real reading certainly needs real books. By taking up reading, children gain access to a richness of magic of language no coursebook can ever offer.
2. We don't need that every child in the classroom has a copy of it. Just a single copy is enough for the teacher to read aloud the stories to the children gathered in a circle

Source: Own elaboration

## Task 4. Checklist phase 2

1. **I have learnt how to organise my presentation so that it makes sense.**
   a. Yes
   b. No
2. **I can identify the different language structures in a text.**
   a. Yes
   b. No

**3. I can identify the structure of a text.**
   a. Yes
   b. No

### *Phase 3: Language tips when creating your presentation*

The main learning aim of this phase is for students to focus on the language structures and to provide essential language tips and discursive skills to create a good presentation.

Phase 3 will be completed in one hour and a half through three different tasks:

- Task 5 is a practice task for students to learn how to create an introduction (reading and writing activity).
- Task 6 is also a practice task for students to respond to difficult situations (reading and writing activity).
- Task 7 is a checklist to assess understanding (reading activity).

In the first practice task (task 5), several examples of signpost language for introductions will be given (see the material 'Writing an introduction'). However, these phrases are written in a non-appropriate way, so students should rephrase them to make them suitable for presentations. In addition, they are expected to identify the introductory purpose each phrase has. They will be able to check their answer with the samples provided in the answer key.

In task 6, students are presented with a series of problematic situations that can happen when answering questions at the end of their presentation (see 'Handling difficult situations'). The aim of the activity will be for them to think of a solution for each question. After having done that, they will be able to compare their answers with samples provided in the answer key.

Finally, in task 7, students can assess their own learning by checking if they have understood the contents of the phase.

### Task 5. Writing an introduction

*As you will know by now, a crucial part of a presentation is the introduction, and there are certain aims that must be always achieved. Even though writing an introduction may seem hard, it will be a piece of cake if you remember these phrases.*

*In this exercise we are going to work with the signpost language that must be used in introductions. The following sentences are clearly not suitable for giving a presentation.*

- *Can you change them so they are more appropriate?*
- *Can you identify their purpose?*

Materials for Task 5. 'Writing an introduction'

- *Be quiet, please, and listen to what I have to say.*
- *Hi everybody*
- *You should be aware that I'm (name)*
- *I will talk about X, Y and Z.*
- *Why would I pick such an odd subject? Well, I want to...*
- *OK! Everythign understood? Let's move on...*
- *No interruptions. Questions, at the end of my talk.*

## Task 6. Handling difficult situations

*During this module, we have stressed that the audience is likely to ask questions about your presentation. Questions can lead to difficult situations. What is the best way of tackling them?*

*In this exercise you will be given a series of problematic situations, and your aim will be to think of a solution for each of them.*

Materials for Task 6. 'Handling difficult situations'

**What would you do if...**

- There are no questions.
- Many questions are asked at once.
- Questions get monopolized by one person, and it seems that other members of the audience would also like to ask questions.

- A question refers to some information you have already talked about in your presentation.
- A question has nothing to do with your topic.
- Either you do not know or are not completely sure about the answer to a question.
- You disagree with the implications of a comment or question.
- You fail to understand what one of the members of the audience is asking.

## Task 7. Checklist phase 3

1. **I have learnt the essential language tips when creating a presentation.**
   a. Yes
   b. No
2. **I can work with the signpost language used in introductions.**
   a. Yes
   b. No
3. **I know how to respond to different situations and questions.**
   a. Yes
   b. No

### *Phase 4: Summarising the information provided*

The main aim of this phase is to provide students with some tips to capture and highlight the essential information the audience needs to understand in a presentation.

Phase 4 will be completed in 30 minutes through two different tasks:

- Task 8 is a practice task to identify signpost language (listening activity).
- Task 9 is a checklist to assess understanding (reading activity).

In task 8, students will be asked to watch a video entitled ‘Women and risk taking’ and to write down the signpost language they identify in the video. In order to carry out this task, it will be necessary to access the video through the following link: https://www.youtube.com/watch?v=6r9DAyP46l0&ab_channel=LearnEnglishwithKT and to use the material ‘Identifying signpost language’.

In task 9, students can assess their own learning, checking if they have properly understood the contents of the phase.

### Task 8. Identifying signpost language

Read, again, the text that you order in Task 3. Can you identify the signpost language used in this presentation? Write it down in the following text entry box (you can modify it):

| Materials for Task 8. 'Identifying signpost language' |
|---|

| |
|---|
| **Introduction:**<br>–<br>–<br>**Transition:**<br>–<br>–<br>**Others:**<br>–<br>–<br>**Conclusion:**<br>–<br>– |

### Task 9. Checklist phase 4

1. **I can summarise the information provided in a text.**
   a. Yes
   b. No
2. **I can identify the signpost language provided throughout the presentation.**
   a. Yes
   b. No

**3. I can highlight the main ideas when writing my presentation.**
   a. Yes
   b. No

### *Phase 5: Creating your own presentation*

The main aim of this phase is to encourage students to create their own presentation without any guidance and support.

The duration of Phase 5 will vary from between one hour and a half and 2 hours. It will be completed through two different tasks:

- Task 10 is a production task for students to create their own presentation (writing activity).
- Task 11 is a checklist to assess understanding (reading activity).

In task 10, students will create their own presentation related to their preferred subject at university, following all the guidelines learned in this module. They then are asked to record themselves (or just their voice) presenting their work. Finally, they can self-assess their presentation with the assessment grid provided (see 'Creating your own presentation').

Finally, in task 11, students can assess their own learning, checking if they have properly understood the contents of the phase.

### Task 10. Creating your own presentation

Now that you have learned about the language of presentations, it is time for you to create your own. You will have to write a presentation about your preferred subject at university, following all the guidelines learned in this module. Then, record yourself (or your voice) presenting your work.

Below there is an assessment grid. You can use it to prepare and assess your presentation.

Materials for Task 10. 'Creating your own presentation'

| *I can...* | *Yes/No* | *Comments for improvement* |
|---|---|---|
| greet the audience | | |
| introduce myself | | |
| express the purpose of my presentation | | |
| state the structure of the presentation | | |
| handle questions | | |
| refer to different types of visuals | | |
| establish transitions between sections | | |
| conclude my presentation appropriately | | |
| thank the audience and invite questions | | |

**Task 11. Checklist phase 5**

1. **I have been able to create my own presentation.**
   a. Yes
   b. No
2. **I have recorded my own presentation.**
   a. Yes
   b. No
3. **I have checked my presentation with the help of the assessment grid.**
   a. Yes
   b. No
4. **I understand the key language tips for giving a good presentation.**
   a. Yes
   b. No
5. **I have acquired the necessary knowledge to understand and give a good presentation.**
   a. Yes
   b. No

Table 17 shows a rubric that has been developed to assess this module and that can be used as a self-assessment, peer-assessment tool for students as well as an evaluation tool for instructors if the module is taught in a class.

#### 2.2.6.4. Rubric for assessment

**Table 17.** Rubric to assess module 5 'The language of presentations'

| Element | Excellent (4) | Good (3) | Fair (2) | Poor (1) |
|---|---|---|---|---|
| **Content Elements** | | | | |
| Introduction | The student provides an adequate introduction, including these elements: greetings, purpose and structure. | The introduction is adequate, but only two of the basic elements are included. | Only one of the required elements in an introduction is included. | The introduction does not include any of the required elements. |
| Synthesis of information | The information is appropriately synthesised, clearly reflecting the main points of the task. | The information is partly synthesised but not very cohesively. | The information is poorly synthesised, and the main points of the presentation are not very clear. | The information is not synthesised, and the presentation is not coherent. It is not written in the student's own words. |
| Organization of the presentation | It includes an introduction, transitions, and a conclusion, and is supported with visual aids | It includes an introduction, a conclusion and some transition elements, and/or visual aids | It includes only two of the three required elements (introduction, conclusions, transitions and/or visual aids) | It does not include an introduction or a conclusion. Supporting elements are not provided. |
| Content | There is a guiding thread and ideas are properly connected. Main points are clear and well supported. | Main points are somewhat clear, with some support. Contents are clearly structured, with a guiding thread. | Ideas are presented in isolation, making it difficult to see the connection between them. Main points need clarifying and support. The content structure is confusing | It is difficult to see the connection between ideas. Main points are not clear and have no support. There is an inadequate structure of contents. |

| | | | | |
|---|---|---|---|---|
| Conclusion | The student summarises the presentation clearly, with closing structures. If there are final questions, they are handled properly. | The conclusion is mostly adequate, but some key information is missing. If there are final questions, the learner has some trouble answering the final questions. | The conclusion includes only one closing structure but a final summary is not included. If there are final questions, the student has some problems answering them. | There is no conclusion to the presentation, and, if there are final questions, they are not answered coherently. |
| **Language Elements** | | | | |
| Fluency, spontaneity, and pronunciation | The student delivers the presentation with fluency and spontaneity, adapting the speech to the situation, as well as self-correcting his/her non-systematic errors while speaking. The pronunciation is very clear. | The student is able to deliver the presentation with some fluency and spontaneity (with little support from his/her notes). S/he is able to self-correct his/her non-systematic errors. The pronunciation is clear. | The student delivers the presentation with some spontaneity although is not always aware of his/her errors while speaking. The pronunciation could be clearer. | The student is not able to answer questions, and systematic errors are observed while speaking. The pronunciation is not clear. |
| Inclusion of signpost language | A wide variety of signpost language structures are included in the introduction, when referring to visual aids, transition structures and in the conclusion. | Signpost language is included in each of the main parts of the presentation, but some structures are not appropriate. | Few signpost language structures are included. | No signpost language is used. |

### *2.2.7. Module 6: Writing abstracts*

#### **2.2.7.1. Overview and aims**

This module aims to provide students with the fundamental knowledge and tools to write abstracts. Writing abstracts is an important learning skill that students will find very useful at university, especially when producing their own reports and final degree dissertation.

An abstract is a short summary of a completed piece of work (such as a report, dissertation or research paper). If done well, it makes the reader want to learn more about the research, since it reports its aims and outcomes. Weissberg & Buker (1990, p. 184) provide the following definition of what an abstract is: "*The abstract is actually the first section of a report, coming after the title and before the introduction. The abstract provides the reader with a brief preview of the study based on information from the other sections of the report. It is often the last part of the report to be written*". Therefore, abstracts serve two main purposes. First, to help potential readers to determine the relevance of a piece of work for their own research and, secondly, to communicate a writer's key findings to those who do not have time to read the whole report.

This topic will be introduced over four different self-study phases, implementing both theoretical aspects and practical exercises under the principles of self-study and self-assessment. In short, the goal of this module is to provide the necessary knowledge about abstracts, focusing on their structure and the language needed to write them.

The interactive version of the module developed in *Genial.ly* can be accessed here: https://view.genial.ly/606ac8630a2eda0ce859918c/learning-experience-didactic-unit-writing-abstractsmodule

And the introductory video hosted in our *L2EARN* channel in YouTube is also freely available: https://www.youtube.com/watch?v=h0pVQGWcm1M&t=391s

At the end of this module, students will be able to:

- Create their own abstract without any type of guidance or support.
- Learn how to identify and link the main ideas of a longer piece of work.
- Use the correct language structures to write an adequate abstract.
- Self-assess their own performance at the end of each phase.

In addition, students will be able to understand written input as well as produce written output related to the content objectives.

The module is designed to be completed in 3 or 4 hours, so students' workload should not be longer than this. According to the Common European Framework of Reference (CEFR), it is adapted to the B2 level (English), and it will contribute to the development of the following skills: spoken comprehension, written comprehension and written production.

### 2.2.7.2. Learning outcomes

The *language skills (CEFR)* that are going to be dealt with in this module are the following:

1. Comprehension:
   a) Written:
      - Can scan quickly through long and complex texts, locating relevant details.
      - Can understand articles and reports concerned with contemporary problems in which the writers adopt particular stances or viewpoints.
      - Can recognise different structures in discursive text: contrasting arguments, problem-solution presentation and cause-effect relationships.

   b) Spoken:
      - Can follow detailed directions.
      - Can understand recordings in the standard form of the language likely to be encountered in social, professional or academic life and identify speaker viewpoints and attitudes as well as the information content.

2. Production:

   a) Written:
      - Can write straightforward, detailed descriptions on a range of familiar subjects within his/her field of interest.
      - Can write short, simple essays on topics of interest.
      - Can synthesise information and arguments from a number of sources.

In this module, we will also work on the following *functions*:

- Summarising information.
- Recapping information.

And the main *language focus* will be:

- Metadiscourse markers.

### 2.2.7.3. Contents: Phases and tasks

Table 18 shows the activities that are going to be carried out in the module.

**Table 18.** List of activities for module 6 'Writing Abstracts'

| Phase | Aim | Tasks | Description | Time | Typology |
|---|---|---|---|---|---|
| Phase 1 | To give an introduction to what abstracts are and how to write them. | Task 1: video and questionnaire. | *Presentation task:* becoming familiar with abstracts. | 20' | Listening |
| | | Task 2: checklist | *Assessment task:* perception checklist. | 5' | Reading |
| Phase 2 | To work with the main components of abstracts, identifying them, and analysing their purpose. | Task 3: ordering an abstract. | *Practice task:* indicating the order of several extracts to create an abstract. | 15' | Reading |
| | | Task 4: analysing an abstract. | *Practice task:* identifying the main components of an abstract. | 20' | Reading |
| | | Task 5: reducing an abstract. | *Production task*: students write a reduced version of a given abstract. | 30' | Writing |
| | | Task 6: checklist. | *Assessment task:* perception checklist. | 5' | Reading |

**Table 18.** Continued

| Phase | Aim | Tasks | Description | Time | Typology |
|---|---|---|---|---|---|
| Phase 3 | To learn the language needed to write abstract (verb tenses and metadiscourse markers). | Task 7: identifying verb tenses. | *Practice task:* practice with verbs to write each abstract component. | 20' | Reading |
| | | Task 8: metadiscourse markers. | *Practice task:* identifying the metadiscourse markers in an abstract and establishing their purpose | 20' | Reading |
| | | Task 9: checklist. | *Assessment task:* perception checklist. | 5' | Reading |
| Phase 4 | To bring together all the information in the module to start creating abstracts. | Task 10: matching abstracts and titles. | *Practice task:* linking scientific abstracts with their titles. | 20' | Reading and writing |
| | | Task 11: creating your own abstract. | *Production task:* students write their own abstract from a previously worked text. | 30-45' | Reading |
| | | Task 12: checklist. | *Assessment task:* perception checklist. | 5' | Reading |

### *Phase 1: Warm-up. Understanding and writing abstracts*

The main learning aim of this phase is for students to become familiar with the basic aspects of an abstract. Students will explore some strategies for understanding the information provided in an abstract and the language that should be used when writing one.

Phase 1 will be completed in 30 minutes through two different tasks:

- Task 1 is a presentation task for students to become familiar with abstracts (listening activity).
- Task 2 is a checklist to assess understanding (reading activity).

In the presentation task (task 1), students will be asked to watch this module's introductory video (https://www.youtube.com/watch?v=h0pVQGWcm1M&t=391s) and answer a questionnaire comprising five multiple-choice questions.

In task 2, students can assess their own learning by checking if they have properly understood the main ideas presented in the video.

**Task 1. Questionnaire on theoretical video: Becoming familiar with abstracts.**

1. **What is an abstract?**
   a. A short summary of a completed research or a longer piece of work.
   b. A description of a short text.
   c. A framework for presenting the main and supporting ideas of a particular subject.
   d. None of the above.
2. **Which one of these is NOT a characteristic of abstracts?**
   a. It helps potential readers determine the relevance of your paper for their own research.
   b. It concludes your piece of work.
   c. It communicates key findings to those who do not have time to read the whole paper.
   d. It provides the reader with a brief preview of the study based on information from the other sections of the report.
3. **Which are the basic components of an abstract?**
   a. Background, purpose and conclusion.
   b. Background, purpose, aim and results.
   c. Purpose, aim, motivation, method and results.
   d. Background, purpose/aim, method, results and conclusion.
4. **Take a look at this question. Which basic component does it refer to?**
   *What practical, scientific, theoretical or artistic gap does your research fill?*
   a. Method.
   b. Conclusion.
   c. Purpose/aim.
   d. Background.

5. **Which type of language should you use when writing your abstract?**
   a. Metaphors.
   b. Metadiscourse markers.
   c. Long sentences.
   d. None of the above.

**Task 2. Checklist phase 1**

1. **I have learnt what an abstract is.**
   a. Yes
   b. No
2. **I know the main characteristics of abstracts.**
   a. Yes
   b. No
3. **I can distinguish between the main components of abstracts.**
   a. Yes
   b. No
4. **I have learned the language used in abstracts.**
   a. Yes
   b. No

***Phase 2: Focusing on the elements of an abstract***

The main aim of phase 2 is to work with the main components of abstracts, analysing the purpose of each of them. Students will learn how to reduce long abstracts.

Phase 2 will be completed in 1 hour through four different tasks:

- Task 3 is a practice task to learn how to order an abstract (reading activity).
- Task 4 is a practice task to analyse an abstract (reading and writing activity).
- Task 5 is a production task to learn how to reduce an abstract (writing activity).
- Task 6 is a checklist to assess understanding (reading activity).

In task 3, students will order different extracts that form an abstract and name each of them according to its purpose. In the practice task (task 4), students are asked to identify the main components of an abstract. In task 5, students will create a reduced version of a given abstract, combining and deleting some components. Finally, in task 6, students can assess their own learning, checking if they have properly understood the contents of the phase.

The materials needed to complete these three tasks are provided below and answers can be checked in the answer key.

## Task 3. Ordering an abstract

*Indicate the correct order of the sentences in the abstract below. Then, name each of the sentences according to the component they represent.*

| Materials for task 3. 'Ordering an abstract' |
|---|

**Abstract 1**

A. A case study was developed with learners from different backgrounds and schools. These learners were asked to perform the activities of a series of materials, which can be used to analyse the main components of language aptitude.
B. The results of the research were compiled from the answers given by the students in each task, and then compared to the students' marks in language-related areas. The results obtained were examined, focusing on each component separately.
C. The present MA dissertation aims to analyse aptitude as a predictor of foreign language acquisition and successful performance, in settings where foreign languages are the means of instruction, i.e., CLIL contexts.
D. The outcomes suggest that, because the students completed the tasks successfully and have high marks in those subjects related to foreign languages, language aptitude can be a predictor of profitable execution in foreign language acquisition.

Source: Calderón-Poves, C. (2020). *Language aptitude influence on foreign language acquisition* (MA dissertation). University of Extremadura, Spain. Retrieved from: http://hdl.handle.net/10662/11606

## Task 4. Analysing an abstract

- *Identify the sentences in the text below that correspond to the main components in an abstract.*
- *Why do you think each sentence corresponds to that element?*

| Materials for task 4. 'Analysing an abstract' |
|---|

**Abstract 2**

*(i) In recent years, the relevance of lexical competence in SLA has grown in importance together with an interest in the strategies students use to learn vocabulary in different contexts. In one of these contexts, Content and Language Integrated Learning (CLIL), however, most of the attention has been usually placed on the potential increase of learners' vocabulary, while the analysis of the specific strategies learners use has been neglected. (ii) This PhD dissertation explores the development of lexical competence in 138 Extremaduran secondary-school learners following two educational approaches (CLIL vs mainstream EFL), (iii) by measuring their receptive and productive mastery of the 2K and academic vocabulary bands and exploring their use of vocabulary learning strategies. (iv) Results indicate a clear difference between CLIL and EFL learners as regards their selection of VLSs and their vocabulary levels. CLIL learners outperformed EFL learners in the receptive and productive vocabulary tests. Concerning VLSs selection, both groups demonstrated to use different strategies, with CLIL learners selecting significantly more often VLSs related to greater lexical development. (v) The results may help us elucidate how CLIL may (1) influence the way learners face vocabulary learning and (2) relate to other factors such as Instructed Amount of Exposure. The confirmation of the differences between both groups of learners in general and academic vocabulary and the finding that the teaching context affects the way L2 vocabulary is processed, together with the consideration of the potential influence of IAoE in these findings, may facilitate the understanding of some of the most contentious CLIL issues.*

Source: Castellano-Risco, I. (2021). *Learning strategies and vocabulary knowledge: a study of secondary-school learners in Content and Language Integrated Learning programmes.* (PhD dissertation). University of Extremadura, Spain. Retrieved from: https://dehesa.unex.es/handle/10662/11726

## Task 5. Reducing an abstract

*Read again Abstract 2 (provided in task 4). Analyse each sentence for the type of information it contains and write out a reduced version.*

- *How many elements are left in your reduced version?*
- *Can you name them according to their purpose?*

**Task 6. Checklist phase 2**

1. **I know the main components of an abstract.**
   a. Yes
   b. No
2. **I can identify the main elements of different types of abstracts.**
   a. Yes
   b. No
3. **I am able to reduce abstracts.**
   a. Yes
   b. No

***Phase 3: Language used in abstracts***

The main learning aim of phase 3 is for students to learn the language needed to write abstracts. Students will work with different verb tenses and metadiscourse markers.

This phase will be completed in 45 minutes through three different activities:

- Task 7 is a practice task to identify verb tenses (reading and writing activity).
- Task 8 is a practice task to identify metadiscourse markers (reading and writing activity).
- Task 9 is a checklist to assess understanding (reading activity).

In the first practice task (task 7), students will be asked to identify the verbs in an abstract, linking them to the different components of the abstract.

In task 8, students will have to identify the metadiscourse markers (and the components these introduce) in an abstract.

Finally, in task 9, students can assess their own learning, checking if they have properly understood the contents of the phase.

The materials needed to complete these three tasks are provided below and answers can be checked in the answer key.

## Task 7. Identifying verb tenses

- *Identify the verbs in Abstract 3 below and explain which component they introduce. You can use the information from the table as a reference.*

| Materials for task 7. 'Identifying verb tenses' |
|---|

**Abstract 3**

*(1) Project-Based Learning (PBL) is focused on providing a student-centred learning environment through meaningful and active methods encouraged by teachers' supportive techniques. The effect of PBL strategies in the development of different areas and skills has been widely studied, and vocabulary acquisition is described as an aspect that often benefits from this method. (2) Thus, the aim of this study is to measure the influence of PBL in the vocabulary acquisition of 45 CLIL, Pre-Primary students belonging to two different age groups (4 and 5 years of age) that were exposed to a different, two-hour, PBL lesson plan, designed within the EU-funded project 'CLIL for Young European Citizens'. (3) An adaptation of the Picture Vocabulary Size Test (PVST), designed by Anthony and Nation, (2017) was first used to obtain information about students' general vocabulary level in English. Two more tests based on the PVST format were designed and implemented in order to measure the effects of PBL lessons on the acquisition of specific vocabulary. (5) The analysis of the data yielded better scores in the PBL tests than in the general English test and statistically significant differences between the two age groups were also found.*

*Source: Pérez-Valenzuela, A. (2021). Project-Based Learning and vocabulary acquisition in pre-primary CLIL students.* MA dissertation. University of Extremadura, Spain. Retrieved from: https://dehesa.unex.es/handle/10662/11726

<table>
<tr><th colspan="3">Element</th><th>Verbal Tense</th><th>Example</th></tr>
<tr><td colspan="3">1. Background information</td><td>Present tense</td><td>“Interest in X has grown in importance in recent years…”</td></tr>
<tr><td colspan="3">2. Purpose/aim</td><td>Present/past tense</td><td>“This study investigates the relationship between…”</td></tr>
<tr><td colspan="3">3. Method/approach</td><td>Past tense</td><td>“Interviews were conducted…” “Tests were administered to…”</td></tr>
<tr><td rowspan="4">4. Result</td><td colspan="2">Statement of the result</td><td>Past tense</td><td>“The coefficient was found to be significant at…”</td></tr>
<tr><td rowspan="3">Comments on results</td><td>Comparison</td><td>Present tense</td><td>“This is consistent with earlier findings that suggest that…”</td></tr>
<tr><td>Possible explanation</td><td>Modal auxiliary</td><td>“These results can/ may be explained by considering…”</td></tr>
<tr><td>Generalisation</td><td>Tentative verbs in the present tense</td><td>“ X may explain…”</td></tr>
<tr><td colspan="3">Conclusion</td><td>Present tense</td><td>“Therefore, the conclusion is that…”.</td></tr>
<tr><th colspan="5">Other Elements</th></tr>
<tr><td colspan="3">Description of figures</td><td>Present tense</td><td>“Table X summarises the results on…”</td></tr>
</table>

## Task 8. Metadiscourse markers

- *Identify the metadiscourse markers in Abstract 1 (you have the full, ordered version below).*
- *Can you analyse the purpose of each of them?*

## Materials for task 8. 'Metadiscourse markers'

**Abstract 1**

*The present MA dissertation aims to analyse aptitude as a predictor of foreign language acquisition and successful performance, in settings where foreign languages are the means of instruction, i.e., CLIL contexts. A case study was developed with learners from different backgrounds and schools. These learners were asked to perform the activities of a series of materials, which can be used to analyse the main components of language aptitude. The results of the research were compiled from the answers given by the students in each task, and then compared to the students' marks in language-related areas. The results obtained were examined, focusing on each component separately. The outcomes suggest that, because the students completed the tasks successfully and have high marks in those subjects related to foreign languages, language aptitude can be a predictor of profitable execution in foreign language acquisition.*

Source: Calderón-Poves, C. (2020). *Language aptitude influence on foreign language acquisition* (MA dissertation). University of Extremadura, Spain. Retrieved from: http://hdl.handle.net/10662/11606

## Task 9. Phase 3 checklist

1. **I know what verb tenses are used in an abstract.**
   a. Yes
   b. No
2. **I can identify the metadiscourse markers in an abstract.**
   a. Yes
   b. No

### *Phase 4: Creating your own abstracts*

The main aim of phase 4 is for students to bring together all the information in the module to start writing their own abstracts. Students will put into practice the contents learned to create an abstract without guidance or support.

Phase 4 will be completed in 1 hour through three different tasks:

- Task 10 is a practice task for students to link abstracts and titles (reading activity).

- Task 11 is a production task for students to create their own abstract (writing activity).
- Task 12 is a checklist to assess understanding (reading activity).

In task 10, students are asked to link several abstracts with their titles, focusing on the characteristics of each of them.

In task 11, students will have to create an abstract from a report or an article that has been previously studied in one of their subjects at university.

Finally, in task 12, students can assess their own learning, checking if they have properly understood the contents of phase 4.

The materials needed to complete these three tasks are provided below and answers can be checked in the answer key.

### Task 10. Matching abstracts and titles

Try to match abstracts 1, 2 and 3 (you have been working with them in some of the previous tasks) with titles 1–3.

- To which discipline do they relate to?
- Do they share common characteristics?

| Materials for task 10. 'Matching abstracts and titles' |
|---|

- **Abstracts**

See Abstracts 1, 2 & 3 (in tasks 4, 7 & 8 above)

- **Titles**

Title A: *Project-Based Learning and vocabulary acquisition in pre-primary CLIL students*
Title B: *Language aptitude influence on foreign language acquisition*
Title C: *Learning strategies and vocabulary knowledge: a study of secondary-school learners in Content and Language Integrated Learning programmes.*

### Task 11. Writing your own abstract

*Now that you have learnt the main components of abstracts and the language that should be used in them, it is time to create your own.*

*You can either choose an article that you have previously read in one of your subjects at university and write an abstract for it or prepare an abstract for your own research. Remember to follow the tips provided in this module.*

**Task 12. Phase 4 checklist**

1. **I can analyse an abstract, identifying the purpose of each component.**
   a. Yes
   b. No
2. **I can use metadiscourse markers and adequate verb tenses in my abstract.**
   a. Yes
   b. No
3. **I am able to create my own abstract.**
   a. Yes
   b. No

Table 19 shows a rubric that has been developed to assess this module and that can be used as a self-assessment, peer-assessment tool for students as well as an evaluation tool for instructors if the module is taught in a class.

*External sources for materials in this module*

– Calderón, C. (2020). *Language aptitude influence on foreign language acquisition* (MA dissertation). University of Extremadura, Spain. Retrieved from: http://hdl.handle.net/10662/11606
– Castellano-Risco, I. (2021). *Learning strategies and vocabulary knowledge: a study of secondary-school learners in Content and Language Integrated Learning programmes.* (PhD dissertation). University of Extremadura, Spain. Retrieved from: https://dehesa.unex.es/handle/10662/11726
– Pérez-Valenzuela, A. (2021). *Project-Based Learning and vocabulary acquisition in pre-primary CLIL students.* MA dissertation. University of Extremadura, Spain. Retrieved from: https://dehesa.unex.es/handle/10662/11726

### 2.2.7.4. Rubric for assessment

**Table 19.** Rubric to assess module 6 'Writing abstracts'

| **Element** | | | | |
|---|---|---|---|---|
| **Content Elements** | **Excellent (4)** | **Good (3)** | **Fair (2)** | **Poor (1)** |
| Organization of the abstract | Includes background information, an aim or purpose, the procedure or method, results or findings, and conclusions and implications. | It includes only four of the required elements. | It includes only three of the required elements. | It includes less than three of the required elements. |
| Cohesion and coherence | The information is perfectly synthesised, clearly reflecting the main points of the production. | The information is not very clearly synthesised. | The information is poorly synthesised, and the main points of the production are not very clear. | The information is not synthesised, nor is it coherent. |
| **Language Elements** | | | | |
| Reporting verbs | It includes a wide variety of reporting verbs, and each of them has the right function and tense. | It uses only the present and past tenses. | All the abstract is written using only one verbal tense. | The verb tenses do not correspond with the function and elements. |
| Mistakes and format | The format is adequate: the abstract is adapted to the required length (150–200 words) and there are no grammatical mistakes. | Even though the length is adequate, there are some grammatical mistakes or vice versa. | The abstract does not comply with the required length and there are some grammatical mistakes. | The format is not adequate: it is not adapted to the required length (less than 100 words or more than 250) and grammatical mistakes are frequent. |
| Inclusion of metadiscourse markers | A wide variety of metadiscourse markers are included in each of the basic components. | Sufficient metadiscourse markers are included, and they are varied. | Some metadiscourse markers are included, but there is not a variety of them. | Metadiscourse markers barely appear. No linking words are used. |

## 2.3. Answer key

### *2.3.1. Introductory module: Creating outlines*

**Task 1** Questionnaire on the theoretical video **Answer key**

1C, 2A, 3B, 4A, 5C, 6A

**Task 3** Differentiating between the elements of a given text **Model answer**

| **Main Idea** | **Supporting Ideas** | **Details** |
| --- | --- | --- |
| The role of speaking | is overemphasized. | |
| 1. | is used in the teaching-learning process. | Teaching and learning through talk |
| 1. | | Ability to talk about subject content |
| The role of writing | is unrecognized. | Interest in oracy |
| | | Teaching and learning are carried out through talk |
| 1. | involves decision making and effort. | Genre |
| 1. | | Register |
| 1. | allows reflection. | |
| 1. | enhances the learning process. | It displays what students know |
| 1. | | It develops and expands language resources |
| 1. | | It demands a different register (register scaffolding) |

## 2.3.2. Module 1: Concept maps

| **Task 1** | Questionnaire on the theoretical video | **Answer key** |
|---|---|---|

1D, 2A, 3A, 4D, 5C, 6C, 7B

| **Task 4** | Identifying the features of concept maps | **Model answer** |
|---|---|---|

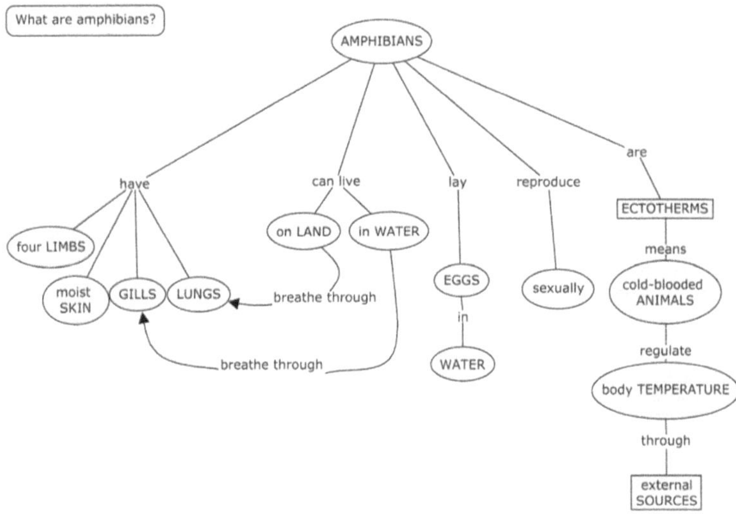


**Figure 19.** Identified concept map 'Amphibians'. Source. Own elaboration

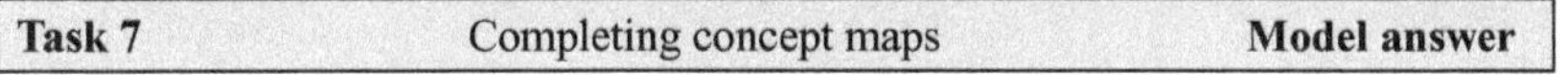

**Task 7** Completing concept maps **Model answer**

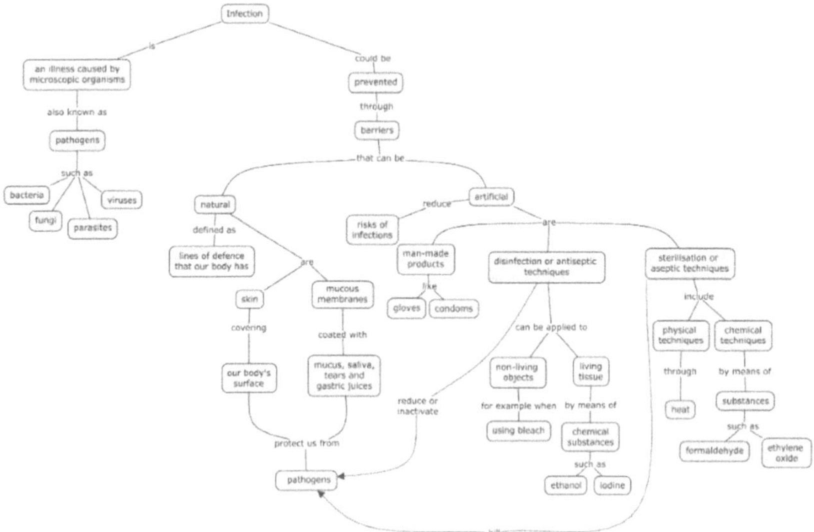


**Figure 20.** Concept map 'Preventing infections' (key). Source: Own elaboration

| **Task 9** | Looking up concepts | **Answer key** |
|---|---|---|

## Activity 1

| **Concrete nouns** | **Abstract nouns** |
|---|---|
| Substance<br>organism<br>secretion<br>germ | Infection<br>effect<br>technique<br>mechanism |

2. **infection**: the process of becoming infected with a disease.
3. **germ**: a form of bacteria that spreads disease among people or animals.
4. **organism**: a living thing such as a person, animal, or plant, especially an extremely small living thing.
5. **technique**: a method of doing something using a special skill that you have developed.
6. **secretion**: a liquid that is produced by a living thing, (or the process of producing this liquid).
7. **effect**: a change that is produced in one person or thing by another.
8. **mechanism**: a system of parts that people think of as working together like the parts of a machine.

## Activity 2

| **Word formation** | | | |
|---|---|---|---|
| **Noun** | **Verb** | **Adjective** | **Adverb** |
| Substance | X | Substantial | Substantially |
| Infection | **Infect** | **Infectious**<br>**Infected**<br>**Infective** | X |
| Germ<br>**Germination** | **Germinate** | X | X |
| Organism<br>**Organ** | **organise/organize** | **Organismic**<br>**organic** | X |
| Technique<br>**Technician** | X | **technical** | **Technically** |

| **Word formation** | | | |
|---|---|---|---|
| Secretion | **Secrete** | **Secretive** | **Secretively** |
| Effect | **Effect** | **Effective**<br>**ineffective** | **Effectively**<br>**Ineffectively** |
| Mechanism | X | **Mechanical** | **Mechanically** |

## Activity 3

1. **secretive**
2. **infect**
3. **technically**
4. **germinate**
5. **organ**
6. **mechanical**
7. **ineffective**

## Task 10 — Building concept maps — Answer key

## Activity 1

| **Giving examples** |
|---|
| For example<br>For instance<br>including<br>Such as<br>To illustrate |

| **Showing purpose** |
|---|
| With the intention of<br>So that<br>In order (not) to |

| **Reasons & causes** |
|---|
| due to<br>because of<br>owing to<br>thanks to<br>caused by<br>following<br>on account of<br>that is why |

| **Results & consequences** |
|---|
| As a result of<br>As a consequence of |

| **Contrast (differences)** |
|---|
| As opposed to<br>Instead of<br>In comparison with<br>Even though<br>But<br>Yet<br>Although<br>In spite of<br>Whereas<br>While |

| **Contrast (similarities)** |
|---|
| Similar to<br>In the same way as |

## Activity 2

1. such as / following / for instance
2. as a result of / as a consequence of / owing to
3. yet / similar to / as opposed to
4. including / with the intention of / in order to

## Activity 3

1. **such**
2. **intention**
3. **consequence / result**
4. **similar**
5. **instead**

| **Task 13** | Creating your own concept map | **Model answer** |
|---|---|---|

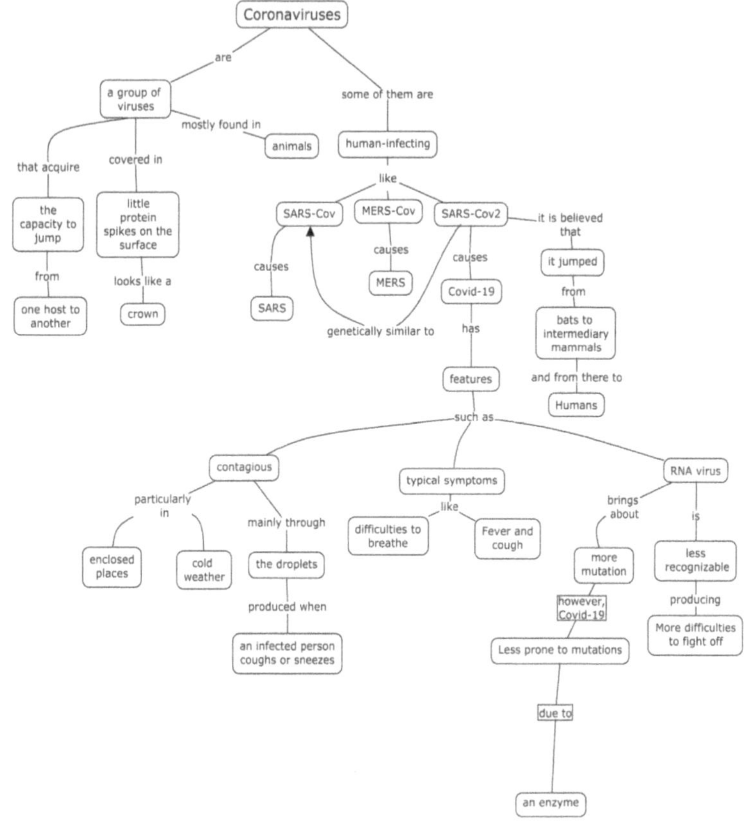


**Figure 21.** Concept map 'Coronaviruses'. Source: Own elaboration

### *2.3.3. Module 2: Writing definitions*

| **Task 1** | Questionnaire on the theoretical video | **Answer key** |
|---|---|---|

1A, 2C, 3C, 4B, 5D, 6D, 7B

| **Task 4** | Identifying the main parts of sentence definitions | **Answer key** |
|---|---|---|

- A **watermelon** is a <u>large round fruit</u> that *has a hard green skin outside and is red with small black seeds inside.*
- A **dictionary** is a <u>reference resource</u> which *provides information about words and their meanings, uses, and pronunciations.*
- **Metal** is a <u>hard element</u> that *exists naturally in the ground or in rock, for example lead, gold, or iron.*
- A **basement** is the <u>part of a building</u> that *is partly or completely below the level of the ground.*
- A **skirt** is a <u>piece of clothing</u> that *covers the lower part of the body and part or all of the legs.*
- A **robot** is a <u>machine</u> that *can do work by itself, often work that humans do.*

| **Bold**: term |
|---|
| <u>Underlined</u>: class |
| *Italics*: specific information |

- **How are these elements joined in the definition?**

The term is usually introduced through an article (normally ‘a’ or ‘the’). It is linked to the class through the verb ‘to be’ and a preposition. Finally, the extra features are added. These are connected to the class through relative clauses (usually with ‘that’ or ‘which’).

- **In your opinion, which definition is the most precise? Why?**

The most precise definitions are those with an accurate class, e.g. ‘watermelon’, ‘dictionary’ or ‘metal’. These concepts provide more information than others which have one-word classes (e.g. ‘robot’).

| Task 6 | Providing precise definitions | **Model answer** |
|---|---|---|

- A **glossary**: a glossary is an alphabetical list, with meanings of the words or phrases in a text that are difficult to understand.
- A **subject**: a subject is an area of knowledge that is studied in school, college, or university.
- **Psychology**: Psychology is the scientific study of the way the human mind works and how it influences behaviour.
- An **outline**: an outline is a framework for presenting the main and supporting ideas of a particular subject or topic.
- **Self-assessment**: self-assessment is a judgment that you make about your abilities, qualities, or actions.
- **English**: English is the language that is natively spoken in the UK, the US, and in many other countries.

| Task 8 | Identifying the main parts of extended definitions | **Answer key** |
|---|---|---|

- **Pollution is a form of environmental contamination resulting from human activity.** *Some common forms of pollution are wastes from the burning of fossil fuels and sewage running into rivers. Even litter and excessive noise can be considered forms of pollution.*
- **A light bulb is an electric light with a wire filament heated until it glows**. *The filament is enclosed in a glass bulb with a vacuum or inert gas to protect the filament from oxidation. Current is supplied to the filament by terminals or wires embeded in the glass. A bulb socket provides mechanical support and electrical connections.*
- **Painting is the practice of applying paint, pigment, colour or other medium to a solid surface.** *The medium is commonly applied to the base with a brush, but other implements, such as knives, sponges, and airbrushes, can be used. In art, the term painting describes both the act and the result of the action (the final work is called 'a painting').*
- **A videotape is magnetic tape used for storing video and usually sound in addition.** *Information stored can be in the form of either an analogue signal or digital signal. Videotape is used in both video tape recorders (VTRs) or, more commonly, videocassette recorders (VCRs) and camcorders.*

- **A flower is the reproductive structure found in flowering plants (plants of the division Magnoliophyta, also called angiosperms).** *The biological function of a flower is to facilitate reproduction, usually by providing a mechanism for the union of sperm with eggs.*

**Bold**: general definition.
*Italics*: specific characteristics.

| Task 11 | Avoiding redundancy | Model answer |
|---|---|---|

- **Paving**: *paving is an area of ground covered with materials such as bricks, blocks of stone, or concrete.*
- **Sight**: *sight is the ability to perceive near objects using the eyes.*
- **Song**: *a song is a short piece of music with words and a melody.*
- **Painting**: *a painting is a picture made using pigments, colours or other medium to a surface.*
- **Erosion**: *erosion is the process during which the surface of the Earth is degraded by the effects of the atmosphere, weather, and human activity.*

| Task 12 | Choosing the most suitable verb | Answer key |
|---|---|---|

- Procrastination **refers** to deliberately putting off one's intended actions.
- The term 'road rage' is **defined** in the Oxford English Dictionary as 'violent anger caused by the stress and frustration of driving in heavy traffic'.
- A study of the geologic record of past seismic activities **is called** paleoseismology.
- The natural increase in temperature as the depth increases **is known** as the geothermal gradient.
- A partitive phrase is a construction that **denotes** part of a whole.
- The activity of visiting interesting places, especially by people on holiday **is named** sightseeing.
- Chakras **refer** to energy points that connect the various bodies each of us inhabit.

- Total government dependency **is defined** as the share of Americans receiving one or more federal benefit payments.
- The share of Americans receiving one or more federal benefit payments **is known** as total government dependency.

### *2.3.4. Module 3: Writing summaries*

| **Task 1** | Questionnaire on the theoretical video | **Answer key** |
|---|---|---|

1A, 2C, 3B, 4C, 5B.

| **Task 3** | Elements of a summary | **Model answer** |
|---|---|---|

(INTRODUCTION): **In this extract from *The Role of Language in CLIL* by Llinares, Morton and Whittaker (2012), the authors highlight the important role of writing when learning in Content and Language Integrated Learning (CLIL) contexts**. Llinares and her colleagues state that (MAIN IDEA): **although a great emphasis is put on spoken language in CLIL lessons, working on writing is essential as it provides learners not only with information but also with models of the language they need to learn**. The authors argue that (SUPPORTING IDEA 1) **writing in a foreign language is a complex, difficult process** that (*DETAILS*) *requires effort on the part of the learners and making decisions at the levels of genre and register*. They report that research shows that (SUPPORTING IDEA 2): **writing fosters reflection** – (*DETAILS*): *leaving a permanent trace in the writer*-, **knowledge creation** – (*DETAILS*) *expanding language resources*-, and **discovery** – (*DETAILS*): *finding the suitable language in the L2*. Finally, the authors (SUPPORTING IDEA 3) **emphasise the importance of helping CLIL learners in the transition from the spoken to the written mode** (*DETAILS*) *through both planned and spontaneous register scaffolding.*

**Questions**

*Is there any irrelevant information?* There is no irrelevant information

*Is there anything missing?* There is no conclusion.

| **Task 4** | Analysing the elements of a summary: Creating an outline | **Model answer** |
|---|---|---|

**Outline**

Importance of WRITING in CLIL contexts

- Writing in CLIL:

1. Essential. It provides learners with information and models
2. Complex. It involves decision-making (genre & register levels)
3. Enriching. It fosters reflection, knowledge creation & discovery
4. It involves a transition from speaking through planned & spontaneous scaffolding

**Question**

*In what ways is it similar to and different from the outlines in the introductory module?*

It contains the key information but it is shorter as it derives from a summary of the original extract.

| **Task 6** | Reporting verbs when referring to authors | **Model answer** |
|---|---|---|

| **Purpose** | **Sentence (S)** |
|---|---|
| **To say indirectly** | – Hume (1738) **suggests/implies** that passions and not reason guide human behaviour |
| **To say directly** | – Newton's first law **states** that an object will not change its motion unless a force acts on it. / **According to** Newton's first law, an object will not change its motion unless a force acts on it. |
| **To say something is true** | – Galilei **claimed / asserted / contended / maintained / declared** that the Earth orbits the Sun.<br>– Einstein's (1905) **shows/demonstrates** the motion of small particles suspended in a stationary liquid, providing empirical evidence for the atomic theory |
| **To give arguments or reasons** | – Martin Luther King **argued** that all races should always be treated equally to white people. |
| **To suggest something is inaccurate** | – Chomsky (1957) **casts doubt on / questions** earlier views about language |

| Purpose | Sentence (S) |
|---|---|
| **To give importance** | – Lakoff & Johnson (1980) **emphasise** / **highlight** / **stress** the importance of metaphor in language and thought. |
| **To refer briefly** | – In her latest book, Littlemore (2019) **mentions** some new research in the field |

| Task 7 | The language of summaries | Model answer |
|---|---|---|

In this extract from *The Role of Language in CLIL* by Llinares et al. (2012), the authors highlight (GIVE IMPORTANCE) the important role of writing when learning in Content and Language Integrated Learning (CLIL) contexts. Llinares, Morton and Whittaker state that (SAY DIRECTLY) although a great emphasis is put on spoken language in CLIL lessons, working on writing is essential as it provides learners not only with information but also with models of the language they need to learn. The authors argue that (GIVE ARGUMENTS OR REASONS) writing in a foreign language is a complex, difficult process that requires effort on the part of the learners and making decisions at the levels of genre and register. They report that (PROVIDE INFORMATION) research shows that writing allows reflection -leaving a permanent trace in the writer-, knowledge creation -expanding language resources-, and discovery -finding the suitable language in the L2. Finally, the authors emphasise (GIVE IMPORTANCE) the importance of helping CLIL learners in the transition from the spoken to the written mode through both planned and spontaneous register scaffolding.

### *2.3.5. Module 4: Reporting data*

| Task 1 | Questionnaire on the video 'Familiarising with graphs' | Answer key |
|---|---|---|

**Answer key:** 1A, 2B, 3C, 4B, 5D, 6D.

| Task 2 | Questionnaire on the video 'Learning how to describe trends' | Answer key |
|---|---|---|

**Answer key:** 1A, 2A, 3C, 4B, 5D, 6D.

| **Task 4** | Working with different types of graphs | **Answer key** |
|---|---|---|

Table 1: a) and d)
Table 2: b)
Table 3: d)
Table 4: e)
Table 5: c)

| **Task 5** | Identifying the elements of a graph | **Answer key** |
|---|---|---|

- **Graph 1**

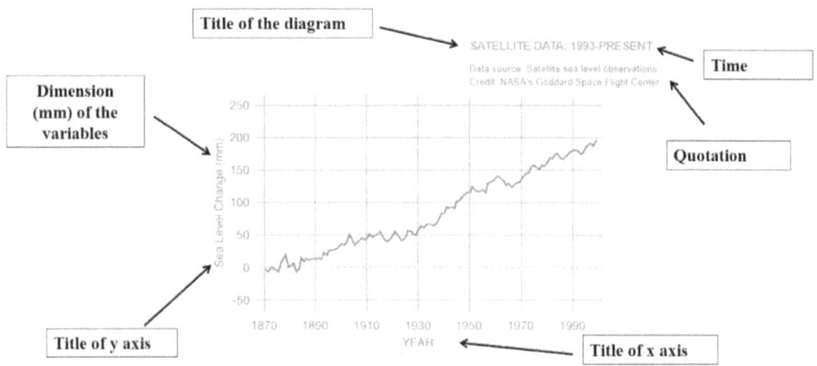


**Figure 22.** Unlabelled Graph 1 (key)

- **Graph 2**

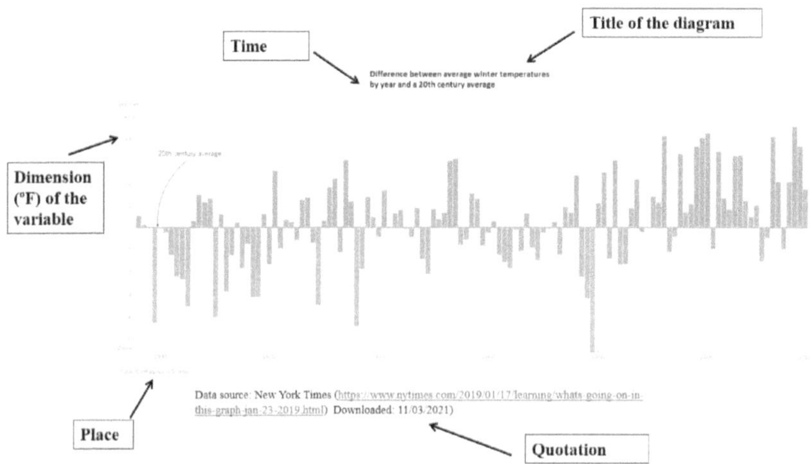


**Figure 23.** Unlabelled Graph 2 (key)

- **Graph 3**

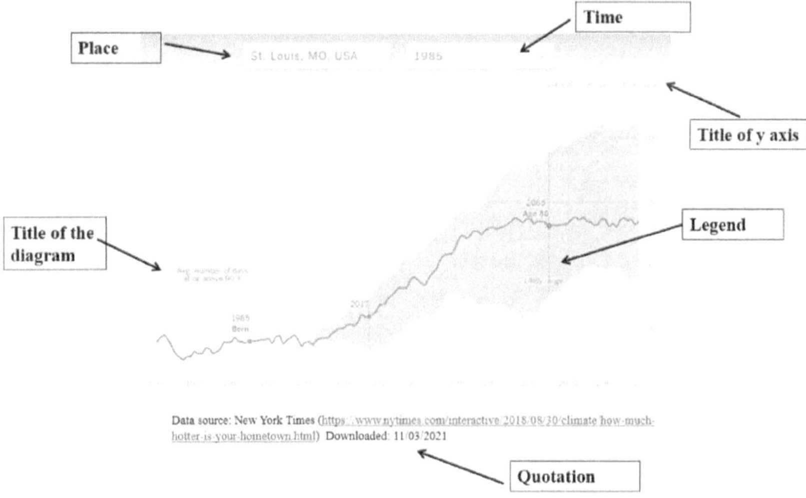


**Figure 24.** Unlabelled Graph 3 (key)

| **Task 6** | Creating your own graph | **Model answer** |
|---|---|---|

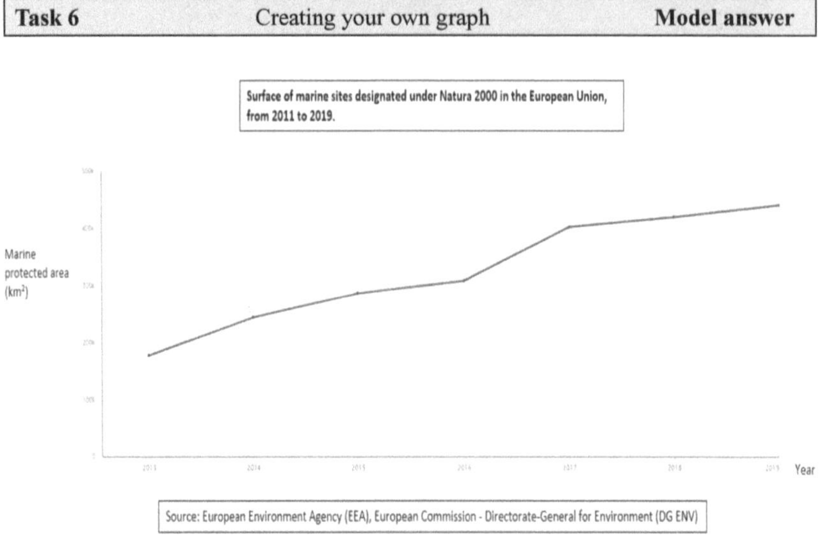


**Figure 25.** Graph from data. Source: European Environment Agency (EEA)

| **Task 8** | Verbs for describing trends | **Answer key** |
|---|---|---|

| | | | | | | | |
|---|---|---|---|---|---|---|---|
| ↑ | Increase | Boom | Go up | Climb | Jump | Grow | Expand |
| ↓ | Decline | Decrease | Go down | Fall | Collapse | | |
| → | Fluctuate | Vary | Stabilise | Stay the same | Level out | | |

| **Task 9** | Nouns for describing trends | **Answer key** |
|---|---|---|

| **Upward trend** | **Verb** | **Noun** |
|---|---|---|
| | To rise | A rise |
| | To increase | An increase |
| | To grow | A growth |
| | To climb | A climb |
| | To boom | A boom |
| | To improve | An improvement |
| | To recover | A recovery |
| | To expand | An expansion |

| **Downward trend** | To fall | A fall |
|---|---|---|
| | To decrease | A decrease |
| | To decline | A decline |
| | To drop | A drop |
| | To collapse | A collapse |
| | To reduce | A reduction |
| | To deteriorate | A deterioration |
| | To weaken | A weakening |
| **Stability** | To level out | A levelling out |
| | To stay the same | - |
| | To stabilize | A stabilisation |
| | To fluctuate | A fluctuation |
| | To vary | A variation |
| | To peak | A peaking |
| | To be volatile | A volatility |
| | To be/remain flat | - |

| **Task 10** | Prepositions for describing trends | **Answer key** |
|---|---|---|

1. What percentage of water is affected by contamination?
2. Pollution rates have risen by two percentage points.
3. The percentage of nuclear energy facilities continues to increase.
4. Farmers only recovered a very small percentage of land.
5. What percentage of green energy sources is used?
6. Average CO2 emissions per km have risen by two percentage points.
7. These figures are expressed as a percentage of the total.
8. Only 40 percent of people bothered to recycle last year.
9. They discovered a 10 percent fall in industrial waste.
10. Over the last years, footprints of consumption fluctuated around/at 20 points.

| **Task 12** | 'Using the vocabulary learned' | **Answer key** |
|---|---|---|

A) In general, the emission rate is relatively stable. In 2010, the emissions rose. However, in 2014 there is a slight decrease, reaching less than 4 m thousand tons of gas emissions.
B) After remaining flat in 100 tonnes of ODS from 1986 to 1989, the ozone substances ratio drastically dropped to around 10 tonnes in 2009. The ratio continued to fall until 2008. Since then, the rate has levelled out.
C) After being relatively stable at around 30 % (EU) and 25 % (EA) between 1990 and 1998, the consumption of fuel experienced a gradual decrease until 2007, when attained a peak of 19 % (EU) and 16 % (EA). Since then, both rates continuously went down to reach 16 % (EU) and 12 % (EA).

| **Task 13** | Linking graphs and statements | **Answer key** |
|---|---|---|

A1, B4, C2, D6, E5, F3

| **Task 14** | How to organise a trend description | **Model answer** |
|---|---|---|

This graph shows the evolution of the unemployment rate in the United States in 1996, measured in percentage. The source is the US Bureau of Labor Statistics, well known and trustable.

There are many ups and downs in this graph. The maximum unemployment rate took place at the beginning of the year and in April and May. The lowest rate occurred in August.

The unemployment rate was more or less stable from January to May, fluctuating between 5.5 and 5.6 %. A sharp fall took place in June, reaching 5.3 %. After that, the rate went up to 5.5 % in July and decreased dramatically again, reaching its lowest point in August (5.1 %). After this, a steady increase happened, reaching 5.4 % in November and December and decreasing to 5.3 % in January.

| **Task 15** | Interpreting a graph | **Answer key** |
|---|---|---|

1. **Elements of the graph:**

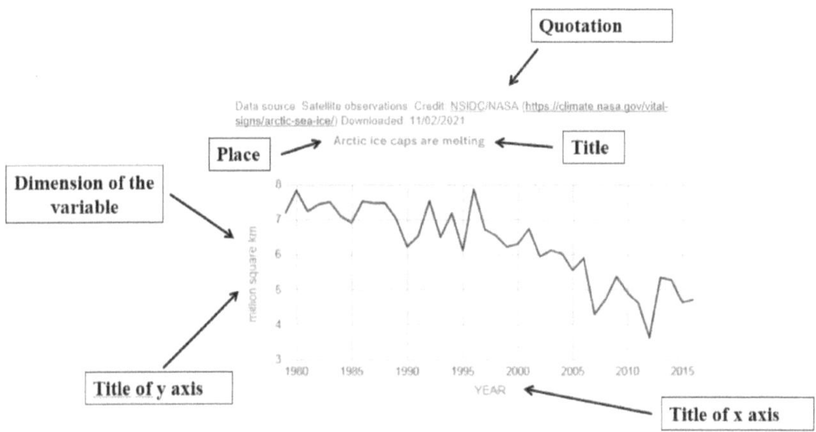


**Figure 26.** Elements of a graph (key)

2. **Short description:** this graph represents the evolution of the melting of the Arctic ice caps, from 1980 to 2015. The surface of ice caps is clearly diminishing, in 1980 being almost 8 million km$^2$, and in 2015 nearly 5 million km$^2$. The surface is at its highest width in 1996, reaching a peak of 8 million km$^2$. Afterwards, it starts dramatically decreasing, dropping to 3.5 million km$^2$ in 2012. After 2012, it rises considerably, levelling off in the following years.

### *2.3.6. Module 5: The language of presentations*

| **Task 1** | Questionnaire on the theoretical video | **Answer key** |
|---|---|---|

1A, 2C, 3A, 4D, 5C, 6D, 7C, 8A, 9A, 10B.

| Task 3 | How to organize a presentation | Answer key |
| --- | --- | --- |

**Extract 1: Introduction**

**Hello, my name is** __________ I am studying a degree in Education (GREETINGS AND INTRODUCING ONESELF) and, **today, I am going to talk about** the benefits of reading for school children. You may have never thought about this topic but over the next 30 minutes or so you will learn some tips to introduce children's literature in your classrooms and I am quite sure that you will find it very interesting (INTRODUCING THE TOPIC). **The main aspects I will be covering in this presentation are the following:**

**First, I will explain** the reasons why 'real' reading needs 'real' books. **Then, I will illustrate how** to use children's book in the classroom. **And, finally, we will have a look at** some of the most popular books for children and talk about their authors (STATING THE STRUCTURE OF THE PRESENTATION)

So, how many of you have used or have thought about using children's book in their classrooms? Please raise your hand if the answer is yes. Ok, so some of you have. (ATTRACTING YOUR AUDIENCE'S ATTENTION WITH A QUESTION)

**Extract 2. Body I**

If you really want to make the most of this practice, you need to plan how to do it considering aspects such as: Should I use real books or reading books? How many books do I need?

If you have ever thought about these questions, it's time you bring children's books into your classroom!

**Extract 3. Body II**

It is important for you to understand that this is a beneficial practice for the kids. In a substantial body of research, scholars have documented the multiple benefits of using children's literature in classrooms. They conclude that literature not only assists children to learn to read but also helps them develop an appreciation for reading as a pleasurable aesthetic experience.

**Going back to** our previous questions:

1. Real reading certainly needs real books. By taking up reading, children gain access to a richness of magic of language no coursebook can ever offer.
2. We don't need that every child in the classroom has a copy of it. Just a single copy is enough for the teacher to read aloud the stories to the children gathered in a circle.

**Extract 4. Body III**

**So now that you know** HOW to do it, **you just need to** select some suitable children's book for your pupils. Some of the best-known and most acclaimed writers are Julia Donaldson (you are surely familiar with 'The Gruffalo'), Eric Carle (everybody knows 'The very hungry caterpillar') or Maurice Sendak and his unique story 'Where the wild things are'.

**Extract 5. Conclusion**

**Let's recap. The most important points we have covered in this presentation are the following** (. . .). (SUMMARISING THE MOST IMPORTANT IDEA/S)A

There are some interesting websites and blogs where you will also find some complementary information and interactive resources.

**Are there any questions?**

**Many thanks for your attention** and I really hope that you consider bringing real children's literature into your classroom. (THANKING YOUR AUDIENCE AND INVITING QUESTIONS)

| **Task 5** Writing an introduction | **Model answer** |
|---|---|

*Now that you have re-written the phrases, take a look at the following examples. Are they similar to yours? Are they more formal than your answers?*

- First words: *Welcome to . . . / Thank you for coming today.*
- Greeting the audience: *Good morning/ Good afternoon/ Good evening.*
- Introducing yourself: *I would like to introduce myself. My name is. . . and I am. . . /*
- Expressing the purpose: *Today, I'd like to talk to you about . . ./ What I'd like to do this morning is to present. . . / My topic/subject today is. . .*
- Giving the structure: *I could start by giving you a brief outline of my presentation. I have divided my talk into four sections. / My presentation will be in two main parts / First, I'll give you an overview of. . .Secondly. . ., Finally. . .*
- Handling questions: *If you have any questions, I'll be happy to answer them.*

| **Task 6** | Handling difficult situations | **Model answer** |
|---|---|---|

- There are no questions
  - *I'd be more than happy to hear your comments and answer any questions that you may have.*
- Many questions are asked at once.
  - *It seems that there are quite a few questions. That's excellent! I'll start from the back and move forward, if that's OK*
- Questions get monopolized by one person, and it seems that other members of the audience would also like to ask questions
  - *Do you mind if I come back to you in a moment? It seems that there are more questions.*
- A question refers to some information you have already talked about in your presentation.
  - *You might recall that in my introduction/discussion/conclusion, I pointed out. . .*
- A question has nothing to do with your topic.
  - *Many thanks for your very interesting comment but I would say that it is not directly related to my topic, perhaps. . .*
- Either you do not know or are not completely sure about the answer to a question

   - *I don't have any actual data on that, but I certainly find your question rather interesting and will definitely look into it.*
- You disagree with the implications of a comment or question
   - *You seem to imply that . . . but in my own view. . .*
- You fail to understand what one of the members of the audience is asking
   - *So, if I understood correctly, you are asking about...*

| **Task 8** | Identifying signpost language | **Model answer** |
|---|---|---|

**Introduction**

- Hello, my name is. . .
- . . .today, I am going to talk about
- . . .over the next 30 minutes or so you will learn. . .

**Transition**

- The main aspects I will be covering in this presentation are the following:
- First, I will explain. . .
- Then, I will illustrate how to. . .
- And, finally, we will have a look at. . .
- Going back to. . .

**Others**

- So now that you know. . .. You just need to. . .

**Conclusion**

- Let's recap.
- The most important points we have covered in this presentation are the following. . .
- Are there any questions?
- Many thanks for your attention.

### *2.3.7. Module 6: Writing abstracts*

| **Task 1** | Becoming familiar with abstracts. Video questionnaire | **Answer key** |
|---|---|---|

1A, 2B, 3D, 4C, 5B

| **Task 3** | Ordering an abstract | **Answer key** |
|---|---|---|

A. 2 Method
B. 3 Results.
C. 1 Aim.
D. 4 Conclusion.

| **Task 4** | Analysing an abstract | **Answer key** |
|---|---|---|

Background: (i). Provides a brief theoretical account on the topic: 'In recent years, the relevance of…', 'In one of these contexts…'

Purpose: (ii). States what is the motivation to do the research: 'This PhD dissertation explores…'

Method: (iii) Explains the specific procedure employed: 'by measuring'

Results: (iv). Explains the results: 'results indicate…'

Conclusion: (v). Summarises the research and states the implications: 'The results may help us elucidate…', 'The confirmation of… may facilitate the understanding of…'

| **Task 5** | Reducing an abstract | **Model answer** |
|---|---|---|

*(i) In recent years, the relevance of lexical competence in SLA has grown in importance together with an interest in the strategies students use to learn vocabulary in different contexts. In one of these contexts, Content and Language Integrated Learning (CLIL), however, most of the attention has been usually placed on the potential increase of learners' vocabulary, while the analysis of the specific strategies learners use*

*has been neglected. (ii) This PhD dissertation explores the development of lexical competence in 138 Extremaduran secondary-school learners following two educational approaches (CLIL vs mainstream EFL), (iii) by measuring their receptive and productive mastery of the 2K and academic vocabulary bands and exploring their use of vocabulary learning strategies. (iv) Results indicate a clear difference between CLIL and EFL learners as regards their selection of VLSs and their vocabulary levels. CLIL learners outperformed EFL learners in the receptive and productive vocabulary tests. Concerning VLSs selection, both groups demonstrated to use different strategies, with CLIL learners selecting significantly more often VLSs related to greater lexical development. (v) The results may help us elucidate how CLIL may (1) influence the way learners face vocabulary learning and (2) relate to other factors such as Instructed Amount of Exposure. The confirmation of the differences between both groups of learners in general and academic vocabulary and the finding that the teaching context affects the way L2 vocabulary is processed, together with the consideration of the potential influence of IAoE in these findings, may facilitate the understanding of some of the most contentious CLIL issues.*

**Final result:**

*(ii) This PhD dissertation explores the development of lexical competence in 138 Extremaduran secondary-school learners following two educational approaches (CLIL vs mainstream EFL), (iii) by measuring their receptive and productive mastery of the 2K and academic vocabulary bands and exploring their use of vocabulary learning strategies. (iv) Results indicate a clear difference between CLIL and EFL learners as regards their selection of VLSs and their vocabulary levels. CLIL learners outperformed EFL learners in the receptive and productive vocabulary tests. Concerning VLSs selection, both groups demonstrated to use different strategies, with CLIL learners selecting significantly more often VLSs related to greater lexical development. (v) The results may help us elucidate how CLIL may (1) influence the way learners face vocabulary learning and (2) relate to other factors such as Instructed Amount of Exposure. The confirmation of the differences between both groups may facilitate the understanding of some of the most contentious CLIL issues.*

**Structure**: (ii) Purpose. (iii) Method. (iv) Results. (v) Conclusion (shortened version).

| **Task 7** | Identifying verb tenses | **Answer key** |
|---|---|---|

(1) Background. Present tense: "**is focused** on…". Present perfect: "**has been** widely **studied**…"
(2) Aim. Present tense: "…the aim of this study **is**…"
(3) Method. Past tense: "An adaptation of … **was** first **used**…" ""Two more tests … **were** and **designed** and **implemented**…"
(5) Stating the results. Present tense: "The analysis of the data **yielded** …", "significant differences … **were** also **found**"

| **Task 8** | Metadiscourse markers | **Answer key** |
|---|---|---|

Metadiscourse markers:

- The present MA dissertation aims to analyse… (purpose/aim)
- A case study was developed… (method)
- These learners were asked to perform… (method)
- The results of the research were… (results)
- The outcomes suggest that… (conclusion)

| **Task 10** | Matching abstracts and title | **Answer key** |
|---|---|---|

Title A: *Project-Based Learning and vocabulary acquisition in pre-primary CLIL students* **(abstract 3)**
Title B: *Language aptitude influence on foreign language acquisition* **(abstract 1)**
Title C: *Learning strategies and vocabulary knowledge: a study of secondary-school learners in Content and Language Integrated Learning programmes* **(abstract 2)**

They are three abstracts from the field of applied linguistics. All of them include the main sections: aim, method and results. Abstract 2 also contains information about the background and conclusions. Abstract 1 has a clear conclusion but does not include a background section whereas in Abstract 3, the conclusions are not explicitly included but there is a detailed background section. Varied metadiscourse markers are used.

# References

Aguilar, M., & Rodríguez, R. (2012). Lecturer and student perceptions on CLIL at a Spanish University. *International Journal of Bilingual Education and Bilingualism,* 15 (2), 183–97.

Alejo González, R. (2018). The place of language in English-medium instruction. Paper presented at the *V Congreso Internacional de Enseñanza Bilingüe 2018*, Badajoz (Spain).

Beelen, J., & Jones, E. (2015). Redefining internationalization at home. In R. Pricopie, J. Salmi, P. Scott, & A. Curai (Eds.), *Redefining internationalization at home* (pp. 67–80). Dordrecht: Springer.

Calderón-Poves, C. (2020). *Language aptitude influence on foreign language acquisition.* MA dissertation. University of Extremadura, Spain.

Castellano-Risco, I. (2021). *Learning strategies and vocabulary knowledge: A study of secondary-school learners in Content and Language Integrated Learning programmes*. PhD dissertation. University of Extremadura, Spain.

Chamot, A. U., & O'Malley, J. M. (1994). *The CALLA handbook: Implementing the cognitive academic language learning approach*. Reading, Massachusetts: Addison-Wesley.

Coelen, R. (2016). A learner-centred internationalisation of higher education. In E. Jones, R. Coelen, J. Beelen, & H. de Wit (Eds.), *Global and local internationalization* (pp. 35–42). Rotterdam: Sense Publishers.

Coelho, M. (2022). *The potential of the CLIL approach with higher education teachers in Portugal: A linguistic needs analysis study at the Polytechnic Institute of Portalegre*. PhD dissertation. University of Extremadura, Spain.

Cummins, J. (2017). BICS and CALP: Empirical and theoretical status of the distinction. In B. Street & S. May (Eds.), *Literacies and language education* (3rd edition, pp. 59–72). Cham: Springer.

Cummins, J. (1979). Cognitive/academic language proficiency, linguistic interdependence, the optimum age question and some other matters. *Working Papers on Bilingualism*, 19, 121–129.

Dafouz, E., & Smit, U. (2016). Towards a dynamic conceptual framework for English-medium education in Multilingual University Settings. *Applied Linguistics*, *37*(3), 397–415.

Dafouz, E., & Smit, U. (2020). *ROAD-MAPPING English Medium Education in the Internationalised University*. Cham: Springer.

Derbentseva, N., Safayeni, F., & Cañas, A. J. (2004). Experiments on the effect of map structure and concept quantification during concept map construction. In *Concept maps: Theory, methodology, technology, proceedings of the first international conference on concept mapping. Pamplona, Spain: Universidad Pública de Navarra*.

de Wit, H., & Deca, L. (2020). Internationalization of higher education, challenges and opportunities for the next decade. In: A. Curaj, L. Deca, & R. Pricopie (Eds.), *European higher education area: Challenges for a new decade*. Cham: Springer

de Wit, H., Hunter, F., Howard, L., & Egron-Polak, E. (2015). *Internationalisation of higher education. European Parliament*. Brussels: Policy Department B. Structural and Cohesion Policies.

Doiz, A., Lasagabaster, D., & Sierra, J. (2013). Globalisation, internationalisation, multilingualism and linguistic strains in higher education. *Studies in Higher Education*, 38(9), 1407–1421.

Fernández Fontecha, A. (2008). CLIL in the foreign language classroom: Proposal of a framework for ICT materials design in language-oriented versions of content and language integrated learning. *Revista Alicantina de Estudios Ingleses*, 21, 317–334.

Flavell, J. H., Miller, P. H., & Miller, S. A. (2002). *Cognitive development* (4th ed.). New Jersey: Prentice-Hall, Inc.

Gustafsson, H. (2020). Capturing EMI teachers' linguistic needs: A usage-based perspective. *International Journal of Bilingual Education and Bilingualism*, 23(9), 1071–1082.

Holliday, A. (1994). *Appropriate methodology and social context*. Cambridge: Cambridge University Press.

Holliday, A., & Cooke, T. M. (1982). An ecological approach to ESP. In A. Waters (Ed.), *Issues in ESP, Lancaster practical papers in English language education* (Vol. 5, pp. 123–1). Lancaster: Pergamon Press.

Holliday, A. R. (1995). Evaluation as cultural negotiation. In *Second PRODESS colloquium: Evaluation in planning and managing language education projects* (pp. 6–11). London: British Council.

Hutchinson, T., & Walters, A. (1987). *English for specific purposes*. Cambridge: Cambridge University Press.

Hyland, K. (2006). *English for academic purposes: An advanced resource book*. London & New York: Routledge.

Knight, J. (1993). Internationalization: Management strategies and issues. *International Education Magazine*, 9(6), 21—22.

Knight, J. (2004). Internationalisation remodeled: Definition, approaches, and rationales. *Journal of Studies in International Education*, 8(1), 5–31.

Knight, J. (2005). *Internationalization of higher education – new directions, new challenges*. Paris: International Association of Universities.

Lasagabaster, D., Doiz, A., Gómez-Lacabex, E., & Kopinska, M. (2021). *Learning history in English language-related materials for students*. Bilbao: Servicio editorial de la Universidad del País Vasco.

Lea. (2004). Academic literacies: A pedagogy for course design. *Studies in Higher Education*, 29(6), 739–756.

Lea, M. (2017). Academic literacies in theory and practice. In B. Street & S. May (Eds.), *Literacies and language education* (3rd edition, pp. 147–158). Cham: Springer.

Llinares, A., Morton, T., & Whittaker, R. (2012). *The roles of language in CLIL*. Cambridge: Cambridge University Press.

Macaro, E. (2018). *English Medium Instruction*. Oxford: Oxford University Press.

Macaro, E. (2022). English Medium Instruction: What do we know so far and what do we still need to find out? *Language Teaching*, 1–14.

Macaro, E., Jiménez-Muñoz, A., & Lasagabaster, D. (2019). The importance of certification of English Medium Instruction teachers in higher education in Spain. *Porta Linguarum*, 32, 103–18.

Mauranen, A. (2012). *Exploring ELF: Academic English shaped by non-native speakers*. Cambridge: Cambridge University Press.

Mehisto, P., Marsh, D., & Frigols, M. J. (2008). *Uncovering CLIL: Content and language integrated learning in bilingual and multilingual education*. Oxford: Macmillan Education.

Montaner-Villalba, S., & Gimeno-Sanz, A. M. (Eds.) (2021). Research in technology-enhanced Content and Language Integrated Learning (CLIL). *VERBEIA. Revista de Estudios Filológicos. Journal of English and Spanish Studies*, 5.

Morell, T., & Volchenkova, K. N. (Eds.) (2021). Special issue: English Medium Instruction (EMI) teacher training in higher education. *Alicante Journal of English Studies / Revista Alicantina de Estudios Ingleses*, 34.

Morgado, M., et al. (2015). *CLIL: Training guide. Creating a CLIL learning community in higher education*. Santo Tirso (Portugal): De Facto Editores.

Morgado, M., et al. (2020). *Interdisciplinary learning and teaching. Digital collaborative methodological guidelines. INCOLLAB* Erasmus+ Strategic Partnership Project (KA2). Project number: 2019-1-CZ01-KA203-061163.

Munby, J. (1978). Communicative syllabus design. Cambridge: Cambridge University Press.

Novak, J. D., & Gowin, D. B. (1984). *Learning how to learn*. Cambridge: Cambridge University Press.

Pecorari, D., & Malmström, H. (2018). At the crossroads of TESOL and English Medium Instruction. *TESOL Quarterly, 52*(3), 497–515.

Pérez-Cañado, M. L. (2021). CLIL-ising EMI: An analysis of student and teacher training needs in monolingual contexts. In C. Hemmi & D. L. Banegas (Eds.), *International perspectives on CLIL* (pp. 171–191). Cham: Palgrave Macmillan.

Pérez-Cañado, M. L. (2020). Addressing the research gap in teacher training for EMI: An evidence-based teacher education proposal in monolingual contexts. *Journal of English for Academic Purposes*, 48, 100927.

Pérez-Cañado, M. L. (2016). Teacher training needs for bilingual education: In-service teacher perceptions. *International Journal of Bilingual Education and Bilingualism*, 19(3), 266–295.

Pérez-Cañado, M. L., & Ojeda-Pinar, B. (2018). *Communicative classroom language for bilingual education teaching "Real English" for CLIL*. Berlin: Peter Lang.

Pérez-Torres, I. (2015). CLIL and web-based instructional strategies: WebQuests and Webtasks. In D. Marsh, M. L. Pérez Cañado, & J. Raéz Padilla (Eds.), *CLIL in action: Voices from the classroom* (pp. 31–46). Cambridge: Cambridge Scholars Publishing.

Pérez-Valenzuela, A. (2021). *Project-based learning and vocabulary acquisition in pre-primary CLIL students*. MA dissertation, University of Extremadura, Spain.

Piquer-Píriz, A. M., Castellano-Risco, I., Alejo-González, R., Martín-Gilete, M., Fielden-Burns, L., Blázquez-López, L., Calderón-Poves, C., & Pérez-Valenzuela, A. (2022). Integración de contenidos y lengua extranjera en la universidad de Extremadura. Guía sobre recursos para el desarrollo de destrezas académicas en la enseñanza-aprendizaje a través del inglés. Cáceres: Servicio de publicaciones de la universidad de Extremadura.

Piquer-Píriz, A. M., & Castellano-Risco, I. (2021). Lecturers' training needs in EMI programmes: Beyond language competence. *Alicante journal of English Studies / Revista Alicantina de Estudios Ingleses,* 34, 83–105.

Piquer-Píriz, A., Morgado, M., & Zverinova, J. (2021). Interdisciplinary collaborative approaches in higher education: Open educational resources for subject and language lecturers. *VERBEIA. Revista de Estudios Filológicos. Journal of English and Spanish Studies*, (5), 81–126.

Safayeni, F., Derbentseva, N., & Cañas, A. J. (2005). A Theoretical Note on Concept Maps and the Need for Cyclic Concept Maps. Journal of Research in Science Teaching, 42(7), 741–766

Schleppegrell, M. J. (2004). *The language of schooling: A functional linguistics perspective.* Mahwah, NJ: Lawrence Erlbaum Associates.

Schleppegrell, M. J. (2006). The challenges of academic language in school subjects. En I. Lindberg & K. Sandwall (Eds.), *Spraket och kunskapen: att lära pa sift andrasprak i skola och högskola* (pp. 47–69). Göteborg: Göteborgs universitet institutet för svenska som andrasprak.

Sursock, A. (2015). *Trends 2015: Learning and teaching in European universities*. Brussels: European University Association.

Swales, J. (1995). English for academic purposes. In P. Byrd (Ed.), *Material Writer's guide* (pp. 124–136). Boston: Heinle & Heinle.

Swales, J. M., & Feak, C. B. (2012). *Academic writing for graduate students: Essential tasks and skills* (3rd edition). Ann Arbor, MI: University of Michigan Press.

Wächter, B., & Maiworm, F. (2014). *English-taught programmes in European higher education. The state of play in 2014.* Bonn: Lemmens Medien

Weissbergs, R., & Buker, S. (1990) *Writing up research*. Englewood Cliffs, NJ: Prentice Hall Regents.

Wilkinson, R. (2018). Content and language integration at universities? Collaborative reflections. *International Journal of Bilingual Education and Bilingualism*, 21(5), 607–15.

# Linguistic Insights

Studies in Language and Communication

This series aims to promote specialist language studies in the fields of linguistic theory and applied linguistics, by publishing volumes that focus on specific aspects of language use in one or several languages and provide valuable insights into language and communication research. A cross-disciplinary approach is favoured and most European languages are accepted.

The series includes two types of books:

- Monographs – featuring in-depth studies on special aspects of language theory, language analysis or language teaching.
- Collected papers – assembling papers from workshops, conferences or symposia.

Each volume of the series is subjected to a double peer-reviewing process.

Vol. 1 Maurizio Gotti & Marina Dossena (eds)
Modality in Specialized Texts. Selected Papers of the 1st CERLIS Conference.
421 pages. 2001. ISBN 3-906767-10-8 · US-ISBN 0-8204-5340-4

Vol. 2 Giuseppina Cortese & Philip Riley (eds)
Domain-specific English. Textual Practices across Communities and Classrooms.
420 pages. 2002. ISBN 3-906768-98-8 · US-ISBN 0-8204-5884-8

Vol. 3 Maurizio Gotti, Dorothee Heller & Marina Dossena (eds)
Conflict and Negotiation in Specialized Texts. Selected Papers of the 2nd CERLIS Conference.
470 pages. 2002. ISBN 3-906769-12-7 · US-ISBN 0-8204-5887-2

Vol. 4 Maurizio Gotti, Marina Dossena, Richard Dury, Roberta Facchinetti & Maria Lima
Variation in Central Modals. A Repertoire of Forms and Types of Usage in Middle English and Early Modern English.
364 pages. 2002. ISBN 3-906769-84-4 · US-ISBN 0-8204-5898-8

***Editorial address:***

Prof. Maurizio Gotti, Emeritus Professor
Università di Bergamo, Dipartimento di Lingue, Letterature e Culture Straniere Piazza Rosate 2, 24129 Bergamo, Italy
Fax: +39 035 2052789, E-Mail: m.gotti@unibg.it

Vol. 5 Stefania Nuccorini (ed.)
Phrases and Phraseology. Data and Descriptions.
187 pages. 2002. ISBN 3-906770-08-7 · US-ISBN 0-8204-5933-X

Vol. 6 Vijay Bhatia, Christopher N. Candlin & Maurizio Gotti (eds)
Legal Discourse in Multilingual and Multicultural Contexts.
Arbitration Texts in Europe.
385 pages. 2003. ISBN 3-906770-85-0 · US-ISBN 0-8204-6254-3

Vol. 7 Marina Dossena & Charles Jones (eds)
Insights into Late Modern English. 2nd edition.
378 pages. 2003, 2007.
ISBN 978-3-03911-257-9 · US-ISBN 978-0-8204-8927-8

Vol. 8 Maurizio Gotti
Specialized Discourse. Linguistic Features and Changing Conventions.
351 pages. 2003, 2005.
ISBN 3-03910-606-6 · US-ISBN 0-8204-7000-7

Vol. 9 Alan Partington, John Morley & Louann Haarman (eds)
Corpora and Discourse.
420 pages. 2004. ISBN 3-03910-026-2 · US-ISBN 0-8204-6262-4

Vol. 10 Martina Möllering
The Acquisition of German Modal Particles. A Corpus-Based Approach.
290 pages. 2004. ISBN 3-03910-043-2 · US-ISBN 0-8204-6273-X

Vol. 11 David Hart (ed.)
English Modality in Context. Diachronic Perspectives.
261 pages. 2003. ISBN 3-03910-046-7 · US-ISBN 0-8204-6852-5

Vol. 12 Wendy Swanson
Modes of Co-reference as an Indicator of Genre.
430 pages. 2003. ISBN 3-03910-052-1 · US-ISBN 0-8204-6855-X

Vol. 13 Gina Poncini
Discursive Strategies in Multicultural Business Meetings.
2nd edition. 338 pages. 2004, 2007.
ISBN 978-3-03911-296-8 · US-ISBN 978-0-8204-8937-7

Vol. 14 Christopher N. Candlin & Maurizio Gotti (eds)
Intercultural Aspects of Specialized Communication.
2nd edition. 369 pages. 2004, 2007.
ISBN 978-3-03911-258-6 · US-ISBN 978-0-8204-8926-1

Vol. 15 Gabriella Del Lungo Camiciotti & Elena Tognini Bonelli (eds)
Academic Discourse. New Insights into Evaluation.
234 pages. 2004. ISBN 3-03910-353-9 · US-ISBN 0-8204-7016-3

Vol. 16 Marina Dossena & Roger Lass (eds)
Methods and Data in English Historical Dialectology.
405 pages. 2004. ISBN 3-03910-362-8 · US-ISBN 0-8204-7018-X

Vol. 17 Judy Noguchi
The Science Review Article. An Opportune Genre in
the Construction of Science.
274 pages. 2006. ISBN 3-03910-426-8 · US-ISBN 0-8204-7034-1

Vol. 18 Giuseppina Cortese & Anna Duszak (eds)
Identity, Community, Discourse. English in Intercultural Settings.
495 pages. 2005. ISBN 3-03910-632-5 · US-ISBN 0-8204-7163-1

Vol. 19 Anna Trosborg & Poul Erik Flyvholm Jørgensen (eds)
Business Discourse. Texts and Contexts.
250 pages. 2005. ISBN 3-03910-606-6 · US-ISBN 0-8204-7000-7

Vol. 20 Christopher Williams
Tradition and Change in Legal English. Verbal Constructions in Prescriptive Texts.
2nd revised edition. 216 pages. 2005, 2007. ISBN 978-3-03911-444-3.

Vol. 21 Katarzyna Dziubalska-Kolaczyk & Joanna Przedlacka (eds)
English Pronunciation Models: A Changing Scene.
2nd edition. 476 pages. 2005, 2008. ISBN 978-3-03911-682-9.

Vol. 22 Christián Abello-Contesse, Rubén Chacón-Beltrán, M. Dolores López-Jiménez & M. Mar Torreblanca-López (eds)
Age in L2 Acquisition and Teaching.
214 pages. 2006. ISBN 3-03910-668-6 · US-ISBN 0-8204-7174-7

Vol. 23 Vijay K. Bhatia, Maurizio Gotti, Jan Engberg & Dorothee Heller (eds)
Vagueness in Normative Texts.
474 pages. 2005. ISBN 3-03910-653-8 · US-ISBN 0-8204-7169-0

Vol. 24 Paul Gillaerts & Maurizio Gotti (eds)
Genre Variation in Business Letters. 2nd printing.
407 pages. 2008. ISBN 978-3-03911-681-2.

Vol. 25 Ana María Hornero, María José Luzón & Silvia Murillo (eds)
Corpus Linguistics. Applications for the Study of English.
2nd printing. 526 pages. 2006, 2008. ISBN 978-3-03911-726-0

Vol. 26 J. Lachlan Mackenzie & María de los Ángeles Gómez-González (eds)
Studies in Functional Discourse Grammar.
259 pages. 2005. ISBN 3-03910-696-1 · US-ISBN 0-8204-7558-0

Vol. 27 Debbie G. E. Ho
Classroom Talk. Exploring the Sociocultural Structure of Formal ESL Learning.
2nd edition. 254 pages. 2006, 2007. ISBN 978-3-03911-434-4

Vol. 28 Javier Pérez-Guerra, Dolores González-Álvarez, Jorge L. Bueno-Alonso & Esperanza Rama-Martínez (eds)
'Of Varying Language and Opposing Creed'. New Insights into Late Modern English.
455 pages. 2007. ISBN 978-3-03910-788-9

Vol. 29 Francesca Bargiela-Chiappini & Maurizio Gotti (eds)
Asian Business Discourse(s).
350 pages. 2005. ISBN 3-03910-804-2 · US-ISBN 0-8204-7574-2

Vol. 30 Nicholas Brownlees (ed.)
News Discourse in Early Modern Britain. Selected Papers of CHINED 2004.
300 pages. 2006. ISBN 3-03910-805-0 · US-ISBN 0-8204-8025-8

Vol. 31 Roberta Facchinetti & Matti Rissanen (eds)
Corpus-based Studies of Diachronic English.
300 pages. 2006. ISBN 3-03910-851-4 · US-ISBN 0-8204-8040-1

Vol. 32 Marina Dossena & Susan M. Fitzmaurice (eds)
Business and Official Correspondence. Historical Investigations.
209 pages. 2006. ISBN 3-03910-880-8 · US-ISBN 0-8204-8352-4

Vol. 33 Giuliana Garzone & Srikant Sarangi (eds)
Discourse, Ideology and Specialized Communication.
494 pages. 2007. ISBN 978-3-03910-888-6

Vol. 34 Giuliana Garzone & Cornelia Ilie (eds)
The Use of English in Institutional and Business Settings.
An Intercultural Perspective.
372 pages. 2007. ISBN 978-3-03910-889-3

Vol. 35 Vijay K. Bhatia & Maurizio Gotti (eds)
Explorations in Specialized Genres.
316 pages. 2006. ISBN 3-03910-995-2 · US-ISBN 0-8204-8372-9

Vol. 36 Heribert Picht (ed.)
Modern Approaches to Terminological Theories and Applications.
432 pages. 2006. ISBN 3-03911-156-6 · US-ISBN 0-8204-8380-X

Vol. 37 Anne Wagner & Sophie Cacciaguidi-Fahy (eds)
Legal Language and the Search for Clarity / Le langage juridique et la quête de clarté. Practice and Tools / Pratiques et instruments.
487 pages. 2006. ISBN 3-03911-169-8 · US-ISBN 0-8204-8388-5

Vol. 38 Juan Carlos Palmer-Silveira, Miguel F. Ruiz-Garrido & Inmaculada Fortanet-Gómez (eds)
Intercultural and International Business Communication.
Theory, Research and Teaching.
2nd edition. 343 pages. 2006, 2008. ISBN 978-3-03911-680-5

Vol. 39 Christiane Dalton-Puffer, Dieter Kastovsky, Nikolaus Ritt & Herbert Schendl (eds)
Syntax, Style and Grammatical Norms. English from 1500–2000.
250 pages. 2006. ISBN 3-03911-181-7 · US-ISBN 0-8204-8394-X

Vol. 40 Marina Dossena & Irma Taavitsainen (eds)
Diachronic Perspectives on Domain-Specific English.
280 pages. 2006. ISBN 3-03910-176-0 · US-ISBN 0-8204-8391-5

Vol. 41 John Flowerdew & Maurizio Gotti (eds)
Studies in Specialized Discourse.
293 pages. 2006. ISBN 3-03911-178-7

Vol. 42 Ken Hyland & Marina Bondi (eds)
Academic Discourse Across Disciplines.
320 pages. 2006. ISBN 3-03911-183-3 · US-ISBN 0-8204-8396-6

Vol. 43 Paul Gillaerts & Philip Shaw (eds)
The Map and the Landscape. Norms and Practices in Genre.
256 pages. 2006. ISBN 3-03911-182-5 · US-ISBN 0-8204-8395-4

Vol. 44 Maurizio Gotti & Davide Giannoni (eds)
New Trends in Specialized Discourse Analysis.
301 pages. 2006. ISBN 3-03911-184-1 · US-ISBN 0-8204-8381-8

Vol. 45 Maurizio Gotti & Françoise Salager-Meyer (eds)
Advances in Medical Discourse Analysis. Oral and Written Contexts.
492 pages. 2006. ISBN 3-03911-185-X · US-ISBN 0-8204-8382-6

Vol. 46 Maurizio Gotti & Susan Šarcević (eds)
Insights into Specialized Translation.
396 pages. 2006. ISBN 3-03911-186-8 · US-ISBN 0-8204-8383-4

Vol. 47 Khurshid Ahmad & Margaret Rogers (eds)
Evidence-based LSP. Translation, Text and Terminology.
584 pages. 2007. ISBN 978-3-03911-187-9

Vol. 48 Hao Sun & Dániel Z. Kádár (eds)
It's the Dragon's Turn. Chinese Institutional Discourses.
262 pages. 2008. ISBN 978-3-03911-175-6

Vol. 49 Cristina Suárez-Gómez
Relativization in Early English (950-1250). the Position of Relative Clauses.
149 pages. 2006. ISBN 3-03911-203-1 · US-ISBN 0-8204-8904-2

Vol. 50 Maria Vittoria Calvi & Luisa Chierichetti (eds)
Nuevas tendencias en el discurso de especialidad.
319 pages. 2006. ISBN 978-3-03911-261-6

Vol. 51 Mari Carmen Campoy & María José Luzón (eds)
Spoken Corpora in Applied Linguistics.
274 pages. 2008. ISBN 978-3-03911-275-3

Vol. 52 Konrad Ehlich & Dorothee Heller (Hrsg.)
Die Wissenschaft und ihre Sprachen.
323 pages. 2006. ISBN 978-3-03911-272-2

Vol. 53 Jingyu Zhang
The Semantic Salience Hierarchy Model. The L2 Acquisition of Psych Predicates
273 pages. 2007. ISBN 978-3-03911-300-2

Vol. 54 Norman Fairclough, Giuseppina Cortese & Patrizia Ardizzone (eds)
Discourse and Contemporary Social Change.
555 pages. 2007. ISBN 978-3-03911-276-0

Vol. 55 Jan Engberg, Marianne Grove Ditlevsen, Peter Kastberg & Martin Stegu (eds)
New Directions in LSP Teaching.
331 pages. 2007. ISBN 978-3-03911-433-7

Vol. 56 Dorothee Heller & Konrad Ehlich (Hrsg.)
Studien zur Rechtskommunikation.
322 pages. 2007. ISBN 978-3-03911-436-8

Vol. 57 Teruhiro Ishiguro & Kang-kwong Luke (eds)
Grammar in Cross-Linguistic Perspective.
The Syntax, Semantics, and Pragmatics of Japanese and Chinese.
304 pages. 2012. ISBN 978-3-03911-445-0

Vol. 58 Carmen Frehner
Email – SMS – MMS
294 pages. 2008. ISBN 978-3-03911-451-1

Vol. 59 Isabel Balteiro
The Directionality of Conversion in English. A Dia-Synchronic Study.
276 pages. 2007. ISBN 978-3-03911-241-8

Vol. 60 Maria Milagros Del Saz Rubio
English Discourse Markers of Reformulation.
237 pages. 2007. ISBN 978-3-03911-196-1

Vol. 61 Sally Burgess & Pedro Martín-Martín (eds)
English as an Additional Language in Research Publication and Communication.
259 pages. 2008. ISBN 978-3-03911-462-7

Vol. 62 Sandrine Onillon
Pratiques et représentations de l'écrit.
458 pages. 2008. ISBN 978-3-03911-464-1

Vol. 63 Hugo Bowles & Paul Seedhouse (eds)
Conversation Analysis and Language for Specific Purposes.
2nd edition. 337 pages. 2007, 2009. ISBN 978-3-0343-0045-2

Vol. 64 Vijay K. Bhatia, Christopher N. Candlin & Paola Evangelisti Allori (eds)
Language, Culture and the Law.
The Formulation of Legal Concepts across Systems and Cultures.
342 pages. 2008. ISBN 978-3-03911-470-2

Vol. 65 Jonathan Culpeper & Dániel Z. Kádár (eds)
Historical (Im)politeness.
300 pages. 2010. ISBN 978-3-03911-496-2

Vol. 66 Linda Lombardo (ed.)
Using Corpora to Learn about Language and Discourse.
237 pages. 2009. ISBN 978-3-03911-522-8

Vol. 67 Natsumi Wakamoto
Extroversion/Introversion in Foreign Language Learning.
Interactions with Learner Strategy Use.
159 pages. 2009. ISBN 978-3-03911-596-9

Vol. 68 Eva Alcón-Soler (ed.)
Learning How to Request in an Instructed Language Learning Context.
260 pages. 2008. ISBN 978-3-03911-601-0

Vol. 69 Domenico Pezzini
The Translation of Religious Texts in the Middle Ages.
428 pages. 2008. ISBN 978-3-03911-600-3

Vol. 70 Tomoko Tode
Effects of Frequency in Classroom Second Language Learning.
Quasi-experiment and stimulated-recall analysis.
195 pages. 2008. ISBN 978-3-03911-602-7

Vol. 71 Egor Tsedryk
Fusion symétrique et alternances ditransitives.
211 pages. 2009. ISBN 978-3-03911-609-6

Vol. 72 Cynthia J. Kellett Bidoli & Elana Ochse (eds)
English in International Deaf Communication.
444 pages. 2008. ISBN 978-3-03911-610-2

Vol. 73 Joan C. Beal, Carmela Nocera & Massimo Sturiale (eds)
Perspectives on Prescriptivism.
269 pages. 2008. ISBN 978-3-03911-632-4

Vol. 74 Carol Taylor Torsello, Katherine Ackerley & Erik Castello (eds)
Corpora for University Language Teachers.
308 pages. 2008. ISBN 978-3-03911-639-3

Vol. 75 María Luisa Pérez Cañado (ed.)
English Language Teaching in the European Credit Transfer System. Facing the Challenge.
251 pages. 2009. ISBN 978-3-03911-654-6

Vol. 76 Marina Dossena & Ingrid Tieken-Boon van Ostade (eds)
Studies in Late Modern English Correspondence. Methodology and Data.
291 pages. 2008. ISBN 978-3-03911-658-4

Vol. 77 Ingrid Tieken-Boon van Ostade & Wim van der Wurff (eds)
Current Issues in Late Modern English.
436 pages. 2009. ISBN 978-3-03911-660-7

Vol. 78 Marta Navarro Coy (ed.)
Practical Approaches to Foreign Language Teaching and Learning.
297 pages. 2009. ISBN 978-3-03911-661-4

Vol. 79 Qing Ma
Second Language Vocabulary Acquisition.
333 pages. 2009. ISBN 978-3-03911-666-9

Vol. 80 Martin Solly, Michelangelo Conoscenti & Sandra Campagna (eds)
Verbal/Visual Narrative Texts in Higher Education.
384 pages. 2008. ISBN 978-3-03911-672-0

Vol. 81 Meiko Matsumoto
From Simple Verbs to Periphrastic Expressions: The Historical Development of Composite Predicates, Phrasal Verbs, and Related Constructions in English.
235 pages. 2008. ISBN 978-3-03911-675-1

Vol. 82 Melinda Dooly
Doing Diversity. Teachers' Construction of Their Classroom Reality.
180 pages. 2009. ISBN 978-3-03911-687-4

Vol. 83 Victoria Guillén-Nieto, Carmen Marimón-Llorca & Chelo Vargas-Sierra (eds)
Intercultural Business Communication and Simulation and Gaming Methodology.
392 pages. 2009. ISBN 978-3-03911-688-1

Vol. 84 Maria Grazia Guido
English as a Lingua Franca in Cross-cultural Immigration Domains.
285 pages. 2008. ISBN 978-3-03911-689-8

Vol. 85 Erik Castello
Text Complexity and Reading Comprehension Tests.
352 pages. 2008. ISBN 978-3-03911-717-8

Vol. 86 Maria-Lluisa Gea-Valor, Isabel García-Izquierdo & Maria-José Esteve (eds)
Linguistic and Translation Studies in Scientific Communication.
317 pages. 2010. ISBN 978-3-0343-0069-8

Vol. 87 Carmen Navarro, Rosa Mª Rodríguez Abella, Francesca Dalle Pezze & Renzo Miotti (eds)
La comunicación especializada.
355 pages. 2008. ISBN 978-3-03911-733-8

Vol. 88 Kiriko Sato
The Development from Case-Forms to Prepositional Constructions in Old English Prose.
231 pages. 2009. ISBN 978-3-03911-763-5

Vol. 89 Dorothee Heller (Hrsg.)
Formulierungsmuster in deutscher und italienischer Fachkommunikation. Intra- und interlinguale Perspektiven.
315 pages. 2008. ISBN 978-3-03911-778-9

Vol. 90 Henning Bergenholtz, Sandro Nielsen & Sven Tarp (eds)
Lexicography at a Crossroads. Dictionaries and Encyclopedias Today, Lexicographical Tools Tomorrow.
372 pages. 2009. ISBN 978-3-03911-799-4

Vol. 91 Manouchehr Moshtagh Khorasani
The Development of Controversies. From the Early Modern Period to Online Discussion Forums.
317 pages. 2009. ISBN 978-3-3911-711-6

Vol. 92 María Luisa Carrió-Pastor (ed.)
Content and Language Integrated Learning. Cultural Diversity.
178 pages. 2009. ISBN 978-3-3911-818-2

Vol. 93 Roger Berry
Terminology in English Language Teaching. Nature and Use.
262 pages. 2010. ISBN 978-3-0343-0013-1

Vol. 94 Roberto Cagliero & Jennifer Jenkins (eds)
Discourses, Communities, and Global Englishes
240 pages. 2010. ISBN 978-3-0343-0012-4

Vol. 95 Facchinetti Roberta, Crystal David, Seidlhofer Barbara (eds)
From International to Local English – And Back Again.
268 pages. 2010. ISBN 978-3-0343-0011-7

Vol. 96 Cesare Gagliardi & Alan Maley (eds)
EIL, ELF, Global English. Teaching and Learning Issues
376 pages. 2010. ISBN 978-3-0343-0010-0

Vol. 97 Sylvie Hancil (ed.)
The Role of Prosody in Affective Speech.
403 pages. 2009. ISBN 978-3-03911-696-6

Vol. 98 Marina Dossena & Roger Lass (eds)
Studies in English and European Historical Dialectology.
257 pages. 2009. ISBN 978-3-0343-0024-7

Vol. 99 Christine Béal
Les interactions quotidiennes en français et en anglais. De l'approche comparative à l'analyse des situations interculturelles.
424 pages. 2010. ISBN 978-3-0343-0027-8

Vol. 100 Maurizio Gotti (ed.)
Commonality and Individuality in Academic Discourse.
398 pages. 2009. ISBN 978-3-0343-0023-0

Vol. 101 Javier E. Díaz Vera & Rosario Caballero (eds)
Textual Healing. Studies in Medieval English Medical, Scientific and Technical Texts.
213 pages. 2009. ISBN 978-3-03911-822-9

Vol. 102 Nuria Edo Marzá
The Specialised Lexicographical Approach. A Step further in Dictionary-making.
316 pages. 2009. ISBN 978-3-0343-0043-8

Vol. 103 Carlos Prado-Alonso, Lidia Gómez-García, Iria Pastor-Gómez &
David Tizón-Couto (eds)
New Trends and Methodologies in Applied English Language Research.
Diachronic, Diatopic and Contrastive Studies.
348 pages. 2009. ISBN 978-3-0343-0046-9

Vol. 104 Françoise Salager-Meyer & Beverly A. Lewin
Crossed Words. Criticism in Scholarly Writing?
371 pages. 2011. ISBN 978-3-0343-0049-0.

Vol. 105 Javier Ruano-García
Early Modern Northern English Lexis. A Literary Corpus-Based Study.
611 pages. 2010. ISBN 978-3-0343-0058-2

Vol. 106 Rafael Monroy-Casas
Systems for the Phonetic Transcription of English. Theory and Texts.
280 pages. 2011. ISBN 978-3-0343-0059-9

Vol. 107 Nicola T. Owtram
The Pragmatics of Academic Writing.
A Relevance Approach to the Analysis of Research Article Introductions.
311 pages. 2009. ISBN 978-3-0343-0060-5

Vol. 108 Yolanda Ruiz de Zarobe, Juan Manuel Sierra &
Francisco Gallardo del Puerto (eds)
Content and Foreign Language Integrated Learning.
Contributions to Multilingualism in European Contexts
343 pages. 2011. ISBN 978-3-0343-0074-2

Vol. 109 Ángeles Linde López & Rosalía Crespo Jiménez (eds)
Professional English in the European context. The EHEA challenge.
374 pages. 2010. ISBN 978-3-0343-0088-9

Vol. 110 Rosalía Rodríguez-Vázquez
The Rhythm of Speech, Verse and Vocal Music. A New Theory.
394 pages. 2010. ISBN 978-3-0343-0309-5

Vol. 111 Anastasios Tsangalidis & Roberta Facchinetti (eds)
Studies on English Modality. In Honour of Frank Palmer.
392 pages. 2009. ISBN 978-3-0343-0310-1

Vol. 112 Jing Huang
Autonomy, Agency and Identity in Foreign Language Learning and Teaching.
400 pages. 2013. ISBN 978-3-0343-0370-5

Vol. 113 Mihhail Lotman & Maria-Kristiina Lotman (eds)
Frontiers in Comparative Prosody. In memoriam: Mikhail Gasparov.
426 pages. 2011. ISBN 978-3-0343-0373-6

Vol. 114 Merja Kytö, John Scahill & Harumi Tanabe (eds)
Language Change and Variation from Old English to Late Modern English.
A Festschrift for Minoji Akimoto
422 pages. 2010. ISBN 978-3-0343-0372-9

Vol. 115 Giuliana Garzone & Paola Catenaccio (eds)
Identities across Media and Modes. Discursive Perspectives.
379 pages. 2009. ISBN 978-3-0343-0386-6

Vol. 116 Elena Landone
Los marcadores del discurso y cortesía verbal en español.
390 pages. 2010. ISBN 978-3-0343-0413-9

Vol. 117 Maurizio Gotti & Christopher Williams (eds)
Legal Discourse across Languages and Cultures.
339 pages. 2010. ISBN 978-3-0343-0425-2

Vol. 118 David Hirsh
Academic Vocabulary in Context.
217 pages. 2010. ISBN 978-3-0343-0426-9

Vol. 119 Yvonne Dröschel
Lingua Franca English. The Role of Simplification and Transfer.
358 pages. 2011. ISBN 978-3-0343-0432-0

Vol. 120 Tengku Sepora Tengku Mahadi, Helia Vaezian & Mahmoud Akbari
Corpora in Translation. A Practical Guide.
135 pages. 2010. ISBN 978-3-0343-0434-4

Vol. 121 Davide Simone Giannoni & Celina Frade (eds)
Researching Language and the Law. Textual Features and Translation Issues.
278 pages. 2010. ISBN 978-3-0343-0443-6

Vol. 122 Daniel Madrid & Stephen Hughes (eds)
Studies in Bilingual Education.
472 pages. 2011. ISBN 978-3-0343-0474-0

Vol. 123 Vijay K. Bhatia, Christopher N. Candlin & Maurizio Gotti (eds)
The Discourses of Dispute Resolution.
290 pages. 2010. ISBN 978-3-0343-0476-4

Vol. 124 Davide Simone Giannoni
Mapping Academic Values in the Disciplines. A Corpus-Based Approach.
288 pages. 2010. ISBN 978-3-0343-0488-7

Vol. 125 Giuliana Garzone & James Archibald (eds)
Discourse, Identities and Roles in Specialized Communication.
419 pages. 2010. ISBN 978-3-0343-0494-8

Vol. 126 Iria Pastor-Gómez
The Status and Development of N+N Sequences in
Contemporary English Noun Phrases.
216 pages. 2011. ISBN 978-3-0343-0534-1

Vol. 127 Carlos Prado-Alonso
Full-verb Inversion in Written and Spoken English.
261 pages. 2011. ISBN 978-3-0343-0535-8

Vol. 128 Tony Harris & María Moreno Jaén (eds)
Corpus Linguistics in Language Teaching.
214 pages. 2010. ISBN 978-3-0343-0524-2

Vol. 129 Tetsuji Oda & Hiroyuki Eto (eds)
Multiple Perspectives on English Philology and History of Linguistics.
A Festschrift for Shoichi Watanabe on his 80th Birthday.
378 pages. 2010. ISBN 978-3-0343-0480-1

Vol. 130 Luisa Chierichetti & Giovanni Garofalo (eds)
Lengua y Derecho. líneas de investigación interdisciplinaria.
283 pages. 2010. 978-3-0343-0463-4

Vol. 131 Paola Evangelisti Allori & Giuliana Garzone (eds)
Discourse, Identities and Genres in Corporate Communication.
Sponsorship, Advertising and Organizational Communication.
324 pages. 2011. 978-3-0343-0591-4

Vol. 132 Leyre Ruiz de Zarobe & Yolanda Ruiz de Zarobe (eds)
Speech Acts and Politeness across Languages and Cultures.
402 pages. 2012. 978-3-0343-0611-9

Vol. 133 Thomas Christiansen
Cohesion. A Discourse Perspective.
387 pages. 2011. 978-3-0343-0619-5

Vol. 134 Giuliana Garzone & Maurizio Gotti
Discourse, Communication and the Enterprise. Genres and Trends.
451 pages. 2011. ISBN 978-3-0343-0620-1

Vol. 135 Zsuzsa Hoffmann
Ways of the World's Words.
Language Contact in the Age of Globalization.
334 pages 2011. ISBN 978-3-0343-0673-7

Vol. 136 Cecilia Varcasia (ed.)
Becoming Multilingual.
Language Learning and Language Policy between Attitudes and Identities.
213 pages. 2011. ISBN 978-3-0343-0687-5

Vol. 137 Susy Macqueen
The Emergence of Patterns in Second Language Writing.
A Sociocognitive Exploration of Lexical Trails.
325 pages. 2012. ISBN 978-3-0343-1010-9

Vol. 138 Maria Vittoria Calvi & Giovanna Mapelli (eds)
La lengua del turismo. Géneros discursivos y terminología.
365 pages. 2011. ISBN 978-3-0343-1011-6

Vol. 139 Ken Lau
Learning to Become a Professional in a Textually-Mediated World.
A Text-Oriented Study of Placement Practices.
261 pages. 2012. ISBN 978-3-0343-1016-1

Vol. 140 Sandra Campagna, Giuliana Garzone, Cornelia Ilie & Elizabeth Rowley-Jolivet (eds)
Evolving Genres in Web-mediated Communication.
337 pages. 2012. ISBN 978-3-0343-1013-0

Vol. 141 Edith Esch & Martin Solly (eds)
The Sociolinguistics of Language Education in International Contexts.
263 pages. 2012. ISBN 978-3-0343-1009-3

Vol. 142 Forthcoming.

Vol. 143 David Tizón-Couto
Left Dislocation in English. A Functional-Discoursal Approach.
416 pages. 2012. ISBN 978-3-0343-1037-6

Vol. 144 Margrethe Petersen & Jan Engberg (eds)
Current Trends in LSP Research. Aims and Methods.
323 pages. 2011. ISBN 978-3-0343-1054-3

Vol. 145 David Tizón-Couto, Beatriz Tizón-Couto, Iria Pastor-Gómez & Paula Rodríguez-Puente (eds)
New Trends and Methodologies in Applied English Language Research II.
Studies in Language Variation, Meaning and Learning.
283 pages. 2012. ISBN 978-3-0343-1061-1

Vol. 146 Rita Salvi & Hiromasa Tanaka (eds)
Intercultural Interactions in Business and Management.
306 pages. 2011. ISBN 978-3-0343-1039-0

Vol. 147 Francesco Straniero Sergio & Caterina Falbo (eds)
Breaking Ground in Corpus-based Interpreting Studies.
254 pages. 2012. ISBN 978-3-0343-1071-0

Vol. 148 Forthcoming.

Vol. 149 Vijay K. Bhatia & Paola Evangelisti Allori (eds)
Discourse and Identity in the Professions. Legal, Corporate and Institutional Citizenship.
352 pages. 2011. ISBN 978-3-0343-1079-6

Vol. 150 Maurizio Gotti (ed.)
Academic Identity Traits. A Corpus-Based Investigation.
363 pages. 2012. ISBN 978-3-0343-1141-0

Vol. 151 Priscilla Heynderickx, Sylvain Dieltjens, Geert Jacobs, Paul Gillaerts & Elizabeth de Groot (eds)
The Language Factor in International Business.
New Perspectives on Research, Teaching and Practice.
320 pages. 2012. ISBN 978-3-0343-1090-1

Vol. 152 Paul Gillaerts, Elizabeth de Groot, Sylvain Dieltjens, Priscilla Heynderickx & Geert Jacobs (eds)
Researching Discourse in Business Genres. Cases and Corpora.
215 pages. 2012. ISBN 978-3-0343-1092-5

Vol. 153 Yongyan Zheng
Dynamic Vocabulary Development in a Foreign Language.
262 pages. 2012. ISBN 978-3-0343-1106-9

Vol. 154 Carmen Argondizzo (ed.)
Creativity and Innovation in Language Education.
357 pages. 2012. ISBN 978-3-0343-1080-2

Vol. 155 David Hirsh (ed.)
Current Perspectives in Second Language Vocabulary Research.
180 pages. 2012. ISBN 978-3-0343-1108-3

Vol. 156 Seiji Shinkawa
Unhistorical Gender Assignment in Lahamon's *Brut*. A Case Study of a Late Stage in the Development of Grammatical Gender toward its Ultimate Loss.
186 pages. 2012. ISBN 978-3-0343-1124-3

Vol. 157 Yeonkwon Jung
Basics of Organizational Writing: A Critical Reading Approach.
151 pages. 2014. ISBN 978-3-0343-1137-3.

Vol. 158 Bárbara Eizaga Rebollar (ed.)
Studies in Linguistics and Cognition.
301 pages. 2012. ISBN 978-3-0343-1138-0

Vol. 159 Giuliana Garzone, Paola Catenaccio, Chiara Degano (eds)
Genre Change in the Contemporary World. Short-term Diachronic Perspectives.
329 pages. 2012. ISBN 978-3-0343-1214-1

Vol. 160 Carol Berkenkotter, Vijay K. Bhatia & Maurizio Gotti (eds)
Insights into Academic Genres.
468 pages. 2012. ISBN 978-3-0343-1211-0

Vol. 161 Beatriz Tizón-Couto
Clausal Complements in Native and Learner Spoken English. A corpus-based study with Lindsei and Vicolse. 357 pages. 2013. ISBN 978-3-0343-1184-7

Vol. 162 Patrizia Anesa
Jury Trials and the Popularization of Legal Language. A Discourse Analytical Approach.
247 pages. 2012. ISBN 978-3-0343-1231-8

Vol. 163 David Hirsh
Endangered Languages, Knowledge Systems and Belief Systems.
153 pages. 2013. ISBN 978-3-0343-1232-5

Vol. 164 Eugenia Sainz (ed.)
De la estructura de la frase al tejido del discurso. Estudios contrastivos español/italiano.
305 pages. 2014. ISBN 978-3-0343-1253-0

Vol. 165 Julia Bamford, Franca Poppi & Davide Mazzi (eds)
Space, Place and the Discursive Construction of Identity.
367 pages. 2014. ISBN 978-3-0343-1249-3

Vol. 166 Rita Salvi & Janet Bowker (eds)
Space, Time and the Construction of Identity.
Discursive Indexicality in Cultural, Institutional and Professional Fields.
324 pages. 2013. ISBN 978-3-0343-1254-7

Vol. 167 Shunji Yamazaki & Robert Sigley (eds)
Approaching Language Variation through Corpora. A Festschrift in Honour of Toshio Saito.
421 pages. 2013. ISBN 978-3-0343-1264-6

Vol. 168 Franca Poppi
Global Interactions in English as a Lingua Franca. How written communication is changing under the influence of electronic media and new contexts of use.
249 pages. 2012. ISBN 978-3-0343-1276-9

Vol. 169 Miguel A. Aijón Oliva & María José Serrano
Style in syntax. Investigating variation in Spanish pronoun subjects.
239 pages. 2013. ISBN 978-3-0343-1244-8

Vol. 170 Inés Olza, Óscar Loureda & Manuel Casado-Velarde (eds)
Language Use in the Public Sphere. Methodological Perspectives and Empirical Applications
564 pages. 2014. ISBN 978-3-0343-1286-8

Vol. 171 Aleksandra Matulewska
Legilinguistic Translatology. A Parametric Approach to Legal Translation.
279 pages. 2013. ISBN 978-3-0343-1287-5

Vol. 172 Maurizio Gotti & Carmen Sancho Guinda (eds)
Narratives in Academic and Professional Genres.
513 pages. 2013. ISBN 978-3-0343-1371-1

Vol. 173 Madalina Chitez
Learner corpus profiles. The case of Romanian Learner English.
244 pages. 2014. ISBN 978-3-0343-1410-7

Vol. 174 Chihiro Inoue
Task Equivalence in Speaking Tests.
251 pages. 2013. ISBN 978-3-0343-1417-6

Vol. 175 Gabriel Quiroz & Pedro Patiño (eds.)
LSP in Colombia: advances and challenges.
339 pages. 2014. ISBN 978-3-0343-1434-3

Vol. 176 Catherine Resche
Economic Terms and Beyond: Capitalising on the Wealth of Notions.
How Researchers in Specialised Varieties of English Can Benefit from Focusing on Terms.
332 pages. 2013. ISBN 978-3-0343-1435-0

Vol. 177 Wei Wang
Media representation of migrant workers in China. Identities and stances
198 pages. 2018. 978-3-0343-1436-7

Vol. 178 Cécile Desoutter & Caroline Mellet (dir.)
Le discours rapporté: approches linguistiques et perspectives didactiques.
270 pages. 2013. ISBN 978-3-0343-1292-9

Vol. 179 Ana Díaz-Negrillo & Francisco Javier Díaz-Pérez (eds)
Specialisation and Variation in Language Corpora.
341 pages. 2014. ISBN 978-3-0343-1316-2

Vol. 180 Pilar Alonso
A Multi-dimensional Approach to Discourse Coherence. From Standardness to Creativity.
247 pages. 2014. ISBN 978-3-0343-1325-4

Vol. 181 Alejandro Alcaraz-Sintes & Salvador Valera-Hernández (eds)
Diachrony and Synchrony in English Corpus Linguistics.
393 pages. 2014. ISBN 978-3-0343-1326-1

Vol. 182 Runhan Zhang
Investigating Linguistic Knowledge of a Second Language.
207 pages. 2015. ISBN 978-3-0343-1330-8

Vol. 183 Hajar Abdul Rahim & Shakila Abdul Manan (eds.)
English in Malaysia. Postcolonial and Beyond.
267 pages. 2014. ISBN 978-3-0343-1341-4

Vol. 184 Virginie Fasel Lauzon
Comprendre et apprendre dans l'interaction. Les séquences d'explication en classe
de français langue seconde.
292 pages. 2014. ISBN 978-3-0343-1451-0

Vol. 185 Forthcoming.

Vol. 186 Wei Ren
L2 Pragmatic Development in Study Abroad Contexts
256 pages. 2015. ISBN 978-3-0343-1358-2

Vol. 187 Marina Bondi & Rosa Lorés Sanz (eds)
Abstracts in Academic Discourse. Variation and Change.
361 pages. 2014. ISBN 978-3-0343-1483-1

Vol. 188 Giuditta Caliendo
Rethinking Community. Discourse, Identity and Citizenship in the European Union.
240 pages. 2017. ISBN 978-3-0343-1561-6

Vol. 189 Paola Evangelisti Allori (ed.)
Identities in and across Cultures.
315 pages. 2014. ISBN 978-3-0343-1458-9

Vol. 190 Erik Castello, Katherine Ackerley & Francesca Coccetta (eds).
Studies in Learner Corpus Linguistics. Research and Applications for Foreign Language Teaching and Assessment.
358 pages. 2015. ISBN 978-3-0343-1506-7

Vol. 191 Ruth Breeze, Maurizio Gotti & Carmen Sancho Guinda (eds)
Interpersonality in Legal Genres.
389 pages. 2014. ISBN 978-3-0343-1524-1

Vol. 192 Paola Evangelisti Allori, John Bateman & Vijay K. Bhatia (eds)
Evolution in Genre. Emergence, Variation, Multimodality.
364 pages. 2014. ISBN 978-3-0343-1533-3

Vol. 193 Jiyeon Kook
Agency in Arzt-Patient-Gesprächen. Zur interaktionistischen Konzeptualisierung von Agency
271 pages. 2015. ISBN 978-3-0343-1666-8

Vol. 194 Susana Nicolás Román & Juan José Torres Núñez (eds)
Drama and CLIL. A new challenge for the teaching approaches in bilingual education.
170 pages. 2015. ISBN 978-3-0343-1629-3

Vol. 195 Alessandra Molino & Serenella Zanotti (eds)
Observing Norm, Observing Usage. Lexis in Dictionaries and in the Media.
430 pages. 2015. ISBN 978-3-0343-1584-5

Vol. 196 Begoña Soneira
A Lexical Description of English for Architecture. A Corpus-based Approach.
267 pages. 2015. ISBN 978-3-0343-1602-6

Vol. 197 M Luisa Roca-Varela
False Friends in Learner Corpora. A corpus-based study of English false friends in the written and spoken production of Spanish learners.
348 pages. 2015. ISBN 978-3-0343-1620-0

Vol. 198 Rahma Al-Mahrooqi & Christopher Denman
Bridging the Gap between Education and Employment. English Language Instruction in EFL Contexts.
416 pages. 2015. ISBN 978-3-0343-1681-1

Vol. 199 Rita Salvi & Janet Bowker (eds)
The Dissemination of Contemporary Knowledge in English. Genres, discourse strategies and professional practices.
171 pages. 2015. ISBN 978-3-0343-1679-8

Vol. 200 Maurizio Gotti & Davide S. Giannoni (eds)
Corpus Analysis for Descriptive and Pedagogical Purposes. ESP Perspectives.
432 pages. 2014. ISBN 978-3-0343-1516-6

Vol. 201 Ida Ruffolo
The Perception of Nature in Travel Promotion Texts. A Corpus-based Discourse Analysis.
148 pages. 2015. ISBN 978-3-0343-1521-0

Vol. 202 Ives Trevian
English suffixes. Stress-assignment properties, productivity, selection and combinatorial processes.
471 pages. 2015. ISBN 978-3-0343-1576-0

Vol. 203 Maurizio Gotti, Stefania Maci & Michele Sala (eds)
Insights into Medical Communication.
422 pages. 2015. ISBN 978-3-0343-1694-1

Vol. 204 Carmen Argondizzo (ed.)
European Projects in University Language Centres. Creativity, Dynamics, Best Practice.
371 pages. 2015. ISBN 978-3-0343-1696-5

Vol. 205 Aura Luz Duffé Montalván (ed.)
Estudios sobre el léxico. Puntos y contrapuntos.
502 pages. 2016. ISBN 978-3-0343-2011-5

Vol. 206 Maria Pavesi, Maicol Formentelli & Elisa Ghia (eds)
The Languages of Dubbing. Mainstream Audiovisual Translation in Italy.
275 pages. 2014. ISBN 978-3-0343-1646-0

Vol. 207 Ruth Breeze & Inés Olza (eds)
Evaluation in media discourse. European perspectives.
268 pages. 2017. ISBN 978-3-0343-2014-6

Vol. 208 Vijay K. Bhatia & Maurizio Gotti (eds)
Arbitration Discourse in Asia.
331 pages. 2015. ISBN 978-3-0343-2032-0

Vol. 209 Sofía Bemposta-Rivas, Carla Bouzada-Jabois, Yolanda Fernández-Pena, Tamara Bouso, Yolanda J. Calvo-Benzies, Iván Tamaredo (eds)
New trends and methodologies in applied English language research III. Synchronic and diachronic studies on discourse, lexis and grammar processing.
280 pages. 2017. ISBN 978-3-0343-2039-9

Vol. 210 Francisco Alonso Almeida, Laura Cruz García & Víctor González Ruiz (eds)
Corpus-based studies on language varieties.
285 pages. 2016. ISBN 978-3-0343-2044-3

Vol. 211 Juan Pedro Rica Peromingo
Aspectos lingüísticos y técnicos de la traducción audiovisual (TAV).
177 pages. 2016. ISBN 978-3-0343-2055-9

Vol. 212 Maria Vender
Disentangling Dyslexia. VenderPhonological and Processing Deficit in Developmental Dyslexia.
338 pages. 2017. ISBN 978-3-0343-2064-1

Vol. 213 Zhilong Xie
Bilingual Advantages. Contributions of Different Bilingual Experiences to Cognitive Control Differences Among Young-adult Bilinguals.
221 pages. 2016. ISBN 978-3-0343-2081-8

Vol. 214 Larissa D'Angelo
Academic posters. A textual and visual metadiscourse analysis.
367 pages. 2016. ISBN 978-3-0343-2083-2

Vol. 215 Evelyne Berger
Prendre la parole en L2. Regard sur la compétence d'interaction en classe de langue.
246 pages. 2016. ISBN 978-3-0343-2084-9

Vol. 216 David Lasagabaster and Aintzane Doiz (eds)
CLIL experiences in secondary and tertiary education: In search of good practices.
262 pages. 2016. ISBN 978-3-0343-2104-4

Vol. 217 Elena Kkese
Identifying Plosives in L2 English: The Case of L1 Cypriot Greek Speakers.
317 pages. 2016. ISBN 978-3-0343-2060-3

Vol. 218 Sandra Campagna, Elana Ochse, Virginia Pulcini & Martin Solly (eds)
Languaging in and across Communities: New Voices, New Identities. Studies in Honour of Giuseppina Cortese.
507 pages. 2016. ISBN 978-3-0343-2073-3

Vol. 219 Adriana Orlandi & Laura Giacomini (ed.)
Defining collocation for lexicographic purposes. From linguistic theory to lexicographic practice.
328 pages. 2016. ISBN 978-3-0343-2054-2

Vol. 220 Pietro Luigi Iaia
Analysing English as a Lingua Franca in Video Games. Linguistic Features, Experiential and Functional Dimensions of Online and Scripted Interactions.
139 pages. 2016. ISBN 978-3-0343-2138-9

Vol. 221 Dimitrinka G. Níkleva (ed.)
La formación de los docentes de español para inmigrantes en distintos contextos educativos.
390 pages. 2017. ISBN 978-3-0343-2135-8

Vol. 222 Katherine Ackerley, Marta Guarda & Francesca Helm (eds)
Sharing Perspectives on English-Medium Instruction.
308 pages. 2017. ISBN 978-3-0343-2537-0

Vol. 223 Juana I. Marín-Arrese, Julia Lavid-López, Marta Carretero, Elena Domínguez Romero, Mª Victoria Martín de la Rosa & María Pérez Blanco (eds)
Evidentiality and Modality in European Languages. Discourse-pragmatic perspectives.
427 pages. 2017. ISBN 978-3-0343-2437-3

Vol. 224 Gilles Col
Construction du sens : un modèle instructionnel pour la sémantique.
292 pages. 2017. ISBN 978-3-0343-2572-1

Vol. 225 Ana Chiquito & Gabriel Quiroz (eds)
Pobreza, Lenguaje y Medios en América Latina.
362 pages. 2017. ISBN 978-3-0343-2142-6

Vol. 226 Xu Zhang
English Quasi-Numeral Classifiers. A Corpus-Based Cognitive-Typological Study.
360 pages. 2017. ISBN 978-3-0343-2818-0

Vol. 227 María Ángeles Orts, Ruth Breeze & Maurizio Gotti (eds)
Power, Persuasion and Manipulation in Specialised Genres. Providing Keys to the Rhetoric of Professional Communities.
368 pages. 2017. ISBN 978-3-0343-3010-7

Vol. 228 Maurizio Gotti, Stefania Maci & Michele Sala (eds)
Ways of Seeing, Ways of Being: Representing the Voices of Tourism.
453 pages. 2017. ISBN 978-3-0343-3031-2

Vol. 229 Dino Selvaggi
Plurilingual Code-Switching between Standard and Local Varieties.
A Socio-Psycholinguistic Approach
371 pages. 2018. ISBN 978-3-0343-2663-6

Vol. 230 Anca-Cristina Sterie
Interprofessional interactions at the hospital. Nurses' requests and reports of problems in calls with physicians.
371 pages. 2017. ISBN 978-3-0343-2734-3

Vol. 231 Xiaodong Zhang
Understanding Chinese EFL Teachers' Beliefs and Practices in the Textbook-Based Classroom.
189 pages. 2017. ISBN 978-3-0343-3053-4

Vol. 232 Manuela Caterina Moroni & Federica Ricci Garotti (Hrsg.)
Brücken schlagen zwischen Sprachwissenschaft und DaF-Didaktik.
345 pages. 2017. ISBN 978-3-0343-2667-4

Vol. 233 Dimitrinka Georgieva Níkleva
Necesidades y tendencias en la formación del profesorado de español como lengua extranjera
401 pages. 2017. ISBN 978-3-0343-2946-0

Vol. 234 Juan Santana-Lario & Salvador Valera (Hrsg.)
Competing patterns in English affixation.
272 pages. 2017. ISBN 978-3-0343-2701-5

Vol. 235 Francisco Salgado-Robles
Desarrollo de la competencia sociolingüística por aprendices de español en un contexto de inmersión en el extranjero
241 pages. 2018. ISBN 978-3-0343-2323-9

Vol. 236 Maria Chiara Janner
Sguardi linguistici sulla marca. Analisi morfosintattica dei nomi commerciali in italiano
345 pages. 2017. ISBN 978-3-0343-2667-4

Vol. 237 Bárbara Herrero Muñoz-Cobo & Otman El Azami Zalachi
La primavera del árabe marroquí.
192 pages. 2017. ISBN 978-3-0343-3104-3

Vol. 238 Consuelo Pascual Escagedo
El papel del oyente en la construcción de la conversación espontánea de estudiantes italianos en su interlengua y en su lengua materna
295 pages. 2017. ISBN 978-3-0343-3186-9

Vol. 239 Stefania M. Maci
The MS Digby 133 *Mary Magdalene*. Beyond scribal practices: language, discourse, values and attitudes.
336 pages. 2017. ISBN 978-3-0343-3256-9

Vol. 240 Eliecer Crespo-Fernández
Taboo in Discourse. Studies on Attenuation and Offence in Communication.
326 pages. 2018. ISBN 978-3-0343-3018-3

Vol. 241 Jana Altmanova, Maria Centrella, Katherine E. Russo (eds)
Terminology & Discourse / Terminologie et discours.
424 pages. 2018. ISBN 978-3-0343-2417-5

Vol. 242 Xavier Blanco et Inès Sfar (dir.)
Lexicologie(s) : approches croisées en sémantique lexicale.
442 pages. 2018. ISBN 978-3-0343-3056-5

Vol. 243 Yunfeng Ge
Resolution of Conflict of Interest in Chinese Civil Court Hearings.
A Perspective of Discourse Information Theory.
302 pages. 2018. ISBN 978-3-0343-3313-9

Vol. 244 Carla Vergaro
Illocutionary Shell Nouns in English
322 pages. 2018. ISBN 978-3-0343-3069-5

Vol. 245 Paolo Frassi
L'adjectif en français et sa définition lexicographique.
270 pages. 2018. ISBN 978-3-0343-3394-8

Vol. 246 Suwilai Premsrirat and David Hirsh (eds)
Language Revitalization. Insights from Thailand
328 pages. 2018. ISBN 978-3-0343-3497-6

Vol. 247 Wei Wang
Researching Learning and Learners in Genre-based Academic Writing Instruction
282 pages. 2018. ISBN 978-3-0343-3297-2

Vol. 248 Isusi Alabarte, Alberto & Lahuerta Martínez, Ana Cristina (eds)
La comprensión lectora de lengua extranjera
Estudio de los factores de familiaridad, interés, género y métodos de evaluación
336 pages. 2018. ISBN 978-3-0343-3493-8

Vol. 249 Mercedes Eurrutia Cavero
Approche didactique du langage techno-scientifique
Terminologie et discours
374 pages. 2018. ISBN 978-3-0343-3512-6

Vol. 250 Aurora Ruiz Mezcua (ed.)
Approaches to Telephone Interpretation
Research, Innovation, Teaching and Transference
268 pages. 2018. ISBN 978-3-0343-3330-6

Vol. 251 Morini Massimiliano
A Day in the News
A Stylistic Analysis of Newsspeak
188 pages. 2018. ISBN 978-3-0343-3507-2

Vol. 252 Ignacio Guillén-Galve & Ignacio Vázquez-Orta (eds.)
English as a Lingua Franca and Intercultural Communication
Implications and Applications in the Field of English Language Teaching
414 pages. 2018. ISBN 978-3-0343-2763-3

Vol. 253 Bianca Del Villano
Using the Devil with Courtesy
Shakespeare and the Language of (Im)Politeness
216 pages. 2018. ISBN 978-3-0343-2315-4

Vol. 254 David Hirsh (ed.)
Explorations in Second Language Vocabulary Research
252 pages. 2018. ISBN 978-3-0343-2940-8

Vol. 255 Tania Baumann (ed.)
Reiseführer - Sprach- und Kulturmittlung im Tourismus / Le guide turistiche - mediazione linguistica e culturale in ambito turistico
270 pages. 2018. ISBN 978-3-0343-3402-0

Vol. 256 Ariadna Sánchez-Hernández & Ana Herraiz-Martínez (eds)
Learning second language pragmatics beyond traditional contexts
376 pages. 2018. ISBN 978-3-0343-3437-2

Vol. 257 Albert Bastardas-Boada, Emili Boix-Fuster, Rosa Maria Torrens (eds)
Family Multilingualism in Medium-Sized Linguistic Communities
336 pages. 2019. ISBN 978-3-0343-2536-3

Vol. 258 Yuyang Cai
Examining the Interaction among Components of English for Specific Purposes Ability in Reading. The Triple-Decker Model
296 pages. 2020. 978-3-0343-2913-2

Vol. 259 Catia Nannoni
Participe présent et gérondif dans la presse française contemporaine
176 pages. 2019. ISBN 978-3-0343-3631-4

Vol. 260 Nieves Rodríguez Pérez & Bárbara Heinsch (eds.)
Contextos multilingües. Mediadores interculturales, formación del profesorado de lenguas extranjeras
289 pages. 2019. ISBN 978-3-0343-3768-7

Vol. 261 Giuliana Elena Garzone, Mara Logaldo, Francesca Santulli (eds.)
Investigating Conflict Discourses in the Periodical Press
244 pages. 2020. ISBN 978-3-0343-3668-0

Vol. 262 Laura Nadal
Lingüística experimental y contraargumentación
233 pages. 2019. ISBN 978-3-0343-3791-5

Vol. 263 Claudia Claridge & Merja Kytö (eds.)
Punctuation in Context – Past and Present Perspectives
288 pages. 2019. ISBN 978-3-0343-3790-8

Vol. 264 Maurizio Gotti, Stefania Maci, Michele Sala (eds.)
Scholarly Pathways
530 pages. 2020. ISBN 978-3-0343-3860-8

Vol. 265 Ruth Breeze, Ana M. Fernández Vallejo (eds.)
Politics and populism across modes and media
350 pages. 2020. ISBN 978-3-0343-3707-6

Vol. 266 Jean Marguerite Jimenez
Understanding the Effects of Immediate Electronic Corrective Feedback on Second Language Development
252 pages. 2020. ISBN 978-3-0343-3815-8

Vol. 267 Sergio Rodríguez-Tapia, Adela González-Fernández (eds)
Lenguas y turismo: estudios en torno al discurso, la didáctica y la divulgación
380 pages. 2020. ISBN 978-3-0343-3881-3

Vol. 268 Ana Bocanegra-Valle (ed.)
Applied Linguistics and Knowledge Transfer. Employability, Internationalisation and Social Challenges
344 pages. 2020. ISBN 978-3-0343-3714-4

Vol. 269 Beatrice Garzelli
La traducción audiovisual español-italiano.Películas y cortos entre humor y habla soez
202 pages. 2020. ISBN 978-3-0343-4013-7

Vol. 270 Iván Tamaredo
Complexity, Efficiency, and Language Contact. Pronoun Omission in World Englishes
292 pages. 2020. ISBN 978-3-0343-3902-5

Vol. 271 Silvia Domenica Zollo,
Origine et histoire du vocabulaire des arts de la table. Analyse lexicale et exploitation de corpus textuels
239 pages. 2020. ISBN 978-3-0343-3890-5

Vol. 272 Paola Paissa, Michelangelo Conoscenti, Ruggero Druetta, Martin Solly (eds.)
Metaphor and Conflict / Métaphore et conflit
385 pages. 2021. 978-3-0343-4068-7

Vol. 273 María Martínez-Atienza de Dios,
Entre el léxico y la sintaxis: las fases de los eventos
178 pages. 2021. 978-3-0343-4173-8

Vol. 274 Noelia Castro-Chao,
Argument Structure in Flux. The Development of Impersonal Constructions in Middle and Early Modern English, with Special Reference to Verbs of Desire.
300 pages. 2021. 978-3-0343-4189-9

Vol. 275 Gabriella Carobbio, Cécile Desoutter, Aurora Fragonara (eds.)
Macht, Ratio und Emotion: Diskurse im digitalen Zeitalter / Pouvoir, raison et émotion: les discours à l'ère du numérique
246 pages. 2020. 978-3-0343-4184-4

Vol. 276 Miguel Fuster-Márquez, José Santaemilia, Carmen Gregori-Signes, Paula Rodríguez-Abruñeiras (eds.)
Exploring discourse and ideology through corpora
293 pages. 2021. 978-3-0343-3969-8

Vol. 277 Tamara Bouso
Changes in Argument Structure
The Transitivizing Reaction Object Construction
392. 2021. 978-3-0343-4095-3

Vol. 278 Maria Luisa Maggioni, Amanda Murphy (eds.)
Back to the Future. English from Past to Present
250 pages. 2021. 978-3-0343-4273-5

Vol. 279 Luisa Chierichetti
Diálogos de serie. Una aproximación a la construcción discursiva de personajes basada en corpus
246 pages. 2021. 978-3-0343-4274-2

Vol. 280 Cristina Lastres-López
From subordination to insubordination. A functional-pragmatic approach to if/si-constructions in English, French and Spanish spoken discourse
258 pages. 2021. 978-3-0343-4220-9

Vol. 281 Eleonora Federici, Stefania Maci (eds.)
Gender issues. Translating and mediating languages, cultures and societies
500 pages. 2021. 978-3-0343-4022-9

Vol. 282 José Mateo, Francisco Yus (eds.)
Metaphor in Economics and specialised Discourse
354 pages. 2021. 978-3-0343-4048-9

Vol. 283 Nicholas Brownlees (ed.)
The Role of Context in the Production and Reception of Historical News Discourse
376 pages. 2021. 978-3-0343-4181-3

Vol. 284 Catalina Fuentes Rodriguez, María Ester Brenes Peña, Víctor Pérez Béjar (eds.)
Sintaxis discursiva: construcciones y operadores en español
396 pages. 2021. 978-3-0343-4306-0

Vol. 285 Dominic Stewart
Frequency in the dictionary. A corpus-assisted contrastive analysis of English and Italian
176 pages. 2021. 978-3-0343-4368-8

Vol. 286 Carla Bouzada-Jabois
Nonfinite supplements in the recent history of English
320 pages. 2021. 978-3-0343-4226-1

Vol. 287 Sofía Bemposta Rivas
Verb-governed infinitival complementation in the recent history of English
320 pages. 2021. 978-3-0343-4227-8

Vol. 288 Mirella Agorni
Translating Italy for the Nineteenth Century. Translators and an Imagined Nation in the Early Romantic Period 1816–1830s
180 pages. 2021. 978-3-0343-3612-3

Vol. 289 David Hirsh (ed.)
Research Perspectives in Language and Education
276 pages. 2021. 978-3-0343-4219-3

Vol. 290 Federica Vezzani
Terminologie numérique : conception, représentation et gestion
238 pages. 2022. 978-3-0343-4394-7

Vol. 291 Stefania M. Maci
Evidential verbs in the genre of medical posters. A corpus-based analysis
498 pages. 2022. 978-3-0343-4521-7

Vol. 292 Francisco J. Álvarez-Gil
Stance devices in tourism-related research articles: A corpus-based study.
170 pages. 2022. 978-3-0343-4555-2

Vol. 293 Annalisa Baicchi / Stefania Biscetti (eds.)
The Language of Fashion. Linguistic, Cognitive, and Cultural Insights
190 pages. 2022. 978-3-0343-4428-9

Vol. 294 Ana Maria Piquer-Píriz
E-learning in EMI. Academic language for university students. 200 pages.
2023. 978-3-0343-4589-7

www.ingramcontent.com/pod-product-compliance
Lightning Source LLC
Chambersburg PA
CBHW060804310726
48980CB00002B/228
*9783034345897*